FROM THE PITCHER'S MOUND TO THE BATTER'S BOX— ZANY MOMENTS THAT WILL LIVE FOREVER IN SHAME!

Q. What manager blew a game when he blew his nose?

A. Lou Boudreau of the Cleveland Indians

Q. What was the most lopsided defeat in baseball history?

A. Boston Red Sox 29, St. Louis Browns 4

Q. What player ended his major league career by hitting into a triple play?

A. Joe Pignatano of the New York Mets

Q. What team played four years without having a manager?

A. The 1961–65 Chicago Cubs

Books by Bruce Nash and Allan Zullo

THE BASEBALL HALL OF SHAME:™
  Young Fans' Edition

THE FOOTBALL HALL OF SHAME:™
  Young Fans' Edition

Available from ARCHWAY Paperbacks

THE
BASEBALL
HALL
OF SHAME™

YOUNG FANS' EDITION

BRUCE NASH and ALLAN ZULLO
BERNIE WARD, CURATOR

AN ARCHWAY PAPERBACK
Published by POCKET BOOKS
New York   London   Toronto   Sydney   Tokyo   Singapore

AN ARCHWAY PAPERBACK *Original*

An Archway Paperback published by
POCKET BOOKS, a division of Simon & Schuster Inc.
1230 Avenue of the Americas, New York, NY 10020

ISBN: 0-671-69354-9

First Archway Paperback printing April 1990

10 9 8 7 6 5 4 3 2 1

THE BASEBALL HALL OF SHAME is a registered
trademark of Nash and Zullo Productions, Inc.

AN ARCHWAY PAPERBACK and colophon
are registered trademarks of Simon & Schuster Inc.

Printed in the U.S.A.

IL 5+

To Sean, Nicole, and Natalie—
three All-Stars in any book.

B.N.

To Frankie Linquist—
a young great sport and a future great ballplayer.

A.Z.

ACKNOWLEDGMENTS

We wish to thank Donna Dupuy for her fine editing and the efforts of Lana Thompson. We also extend our thanks to all the thousands of fans, players, sportswriters, and broadcasters who contributed nominations to The Baseball Hall of SHAME.

CONTENTS

Contents

LEADING OFF

It's time to give discredit where discredit is due.

For over a century, baseball has immortalized the home run slugger, the clean-cut all-American, the golden glover, the big-hearted lug, the unstoppable dynasty. But the truth is winners and nice guys and heroes are boring.

Who really makes the grand old game so entertaining, rousing, and exciting? It's the losers, the flakes, the buffoons, the boneheads, and the outrageous. They have given real demeaning to the word baseball. They have brought color to the game—a black eye. These are the true foul balls whose contributions have withstood the detest of time.

Yet where is their niche in the Hall of Fame? Nowhere.

To correct this injustice in sports, we founded The Baseball Hall of SHAME. Cooperstown can have baseball's shining stars. The Hall of SHAME wants baseball's shiners.

The history of our national pastime boasts a rich

heritage of shameful moments both on and off the field. Hall of SHAMERS include teams, players, managers, coaches, owners, general managers, umpires, groundskeepers, and even the fans themselves.

To help us choose the most deserving candidates for Baseball Hall of SHAME dishonors, we made a nationwide appeal in the spring of 1984. We asked fans, sportswriters, broadcasters, and players for nominations. We spread the word on radio from coast to coast and throughout Canada. We went on TV and were interviewed in scores of newspapers and magazines. We visited spring training camps where we received nominations in the bleachers, clubhouses, dugouts, and press boxes. Then we spent weeks sifting through record books, magazines, and faded newspaper accounts.

Not everyone who blundered on or off the field belongs in The Baseball Hall of SHAME. In our judgment, only a small select number of the thousands of bloopers and boners in baseball history met our unique standards for inclusion in the Hall's first induction.

However, we don't intend to stop here. Periodically, we will be considering prospective Hall of SHAMERS from the past and present for enshrinement. If you feel some baseball personality or moment is deserving of such dishonors, we want to know about it. Please send us your nominations of hilarious happenings and wacky incidents. To learn how to submit your picks, turn to page 131.

We want The Baseball Hall of SHAME to be the fans' shrine. We're not out to make fun of baseball. Instead, we want to have fun with the game we all love. This book is more than just the official record of charter membership in The Baseball Hall of SHAME. It's also a way for fans across the country to pay a lighthearted tribute to the national pastime. We have found that superstars and bozos have one thing in common—they all mess up. (It's just that some mess up more than others.)

As you read through this book, we hope you come to the same conclusion we did. We can all identify with—and laugh about—each inductee's shameful moment because each one of us has at one time or another made a mistake.

WELCOME TO THE BIGS!

*Future major leaguers dream about what that
glorious first day in the bigs will be like. Some
see themselves hammering the winning home run
with two out in the bottom of the ninth. Others
imagine leaping high against the fence for a
game-saving catch. That's the fantasy. The real-
ity is that in their diamond debuts they often fall
on their faces. Many disgrace themselves so
badly it haunts them the rest of their careers. And
that can be a whole lot shorter than they
planned. For "The Wackiest Major League Debuts," The Baseball Hall of SHAME inducts the
following:*

HARRY HEITMAN
Pitcher • Brooklyn, N.L. • July 27, 1918

Harry Heitman holds a dishonor no other player can
claim. Hapless Harry is the first inductee into The
Baseball Hall of SHAME—and he deserves it.

Against St. Louis in his very first game, Heitman had barely warmed up when disaster struck. The Cardinals—and everlasting shame—came crashing down on him like a ton of bats. He faced five batters and managed to get only one out. The other four hitters ripped him for two singles and two triples.

Heitman staggered off the mound with a whopping ERA of 108.00. Owning a stat like that, Heitman did the only thing he could. He tossed his glove away and enlisted in the Navy that very afternoon. He never pitched in the majors again.

BRUNO HAAS
Pitcher • Philadelphia, A.L. • June 23, 1915

Fresh out of Worcester Academy where baseball was still a gentleman's game, Bruno Haas learned quickly that the baseball field of honor can be brutal.

Haas was starting against the Yankees in his debut. He strode proudly to the mound in his new Philadelphia uniform. But any similarity between him and a major league pitcher ended there. Haas gave up 15 runs and 11 hits. It wasn't too bad, considering he couldn't get the ball over the plate.

Like a generous circus owner, Haas gave free passes to everyone in pinstripes. By the end of the day he had walked 16 batters, which was a record for a nine-inning game. In case anybody doubted his wildness, he also uncorked three wild pitches.

At the end of the year, Haas vanished from the majors. Some said he just "walked" away.

BILLY HERMAN
Second Baseman ● Chicago, N.L. ● Aug. 29, 1931

Billy Herman can't remember a whole lot about his big league debut. It's just as well.

Billy was thrilled with the chance to break into the starting lineup. He was determined to prove he belonged. Batting against Cincinnati Reds hurler Si Johnson, Billy dug into the batter's box.

Johnson threw and Billy took a tremendous swing. The ball hit the ground in back of the plate. With wicked reverse English, it bounced straight back and smacked Billy right on the head.

So a sterling career that spanned two decades and ended with a .304 lifetime batting average started out in the least noble way possible. Billy Herman was carried off the field on a stretcher—knocked out cold by his own foul ball!

NEW YORK METS
April 11, 1962

The debut of New York's expansion team set the tone for a season in which "Mets" became America's favorite four-letter word.

Actually, trouble began on the eve of opening day in St. Louis. Sixteen Mets got stuck in the Chase Hotel elevator for 20 minutes. It was a sure sign of disaster.

The next day, in their first game ever, the Mets' fortunes plunged straight into the basement. But it

6

Thanks to some bumbling baserunning, two Mets runners wind up on third base at the same time.
AP/WIDE WORLD PHOTOS

wasn't just because they lost 11–4. What made it really pitiful was their first-inning performance.

Cardinal runner Bill White was on third base. New York pitcher Roger Craig looked in for the sign and checked the runner. Then Craig went into his stretch . . . and dropped the ball! Stunned, Craig watched the umpire wave White home.

The Mets had given up the first run in the history of the franchise on a balk!

THE BOTTOM OF THE BARREL

*Some teams belong at the top of the standings.
Others belong in an old Three Stooges movie.
Their pitchers have trouble finding the mound, let
alone home plate. Their hitters get no-hit in batting practice. And their fielders act as if they're
trying out as circus clowns. These teams tumble
straight into the cellar on Opening Day and stay
there. For "The Worst Teams of All Time," The
Baseball Hall of SHAME inducts the following:*

CLEVELAND SPIDERS
1899

The Cleveland Spiders of 1899 were absolutely the
worst team in baseball history.

Wallowing in the basement of the 12-team National League, these laughable losers piled up 134
losses against only 20 wins. It was the all-time lowest
winning percentage—.130. They finished 84 games out
of first. Compared to the Spiders, history's other
lousiest teams seem like pennant contenders.

They were last in runs, doubles, triples, homers, batting average, slugging percentage, and stolen bases. They were outscored by a two-to-one margin—1,252 runs to 529.

The Spiders started their losing habit in the first game of the season. They were squashed 10–1. Six different times they recorded losing streaks of 11 or more games. One day in Brooklyn, they found themselves in an unfamiliar situation. After six innings, they were leading 10–1. Refusing to bow to victory, they pulled out the defeat 11–10.

Losses piled up left and right. Before the end of the first month, manager Lave Cross quit in disgust.

Blame the team's awful record on its owners, brothers Frank and Matthew Robison. They knew very little about baseball. Instead of hiring more talent before the season started, they bought another team—the St. Louis Browns. Then the Brothers Robison went to work dissecting the Spiders.

To make sure the Spiders failed, they shipped their best players to the Browns. One of them was Cy Young, who won 26 games for St. Louis that season. That was 6 more than his former team won all year.

It's a miracle the Spider fielders survived after all the line drives hit off their pitchers. The two "aces" on the staff were Charlie Knepper and Jim Hughey. Each won a measly 4 games and together were responsible for 52 losses.

Even the Spiders' own families wouldn't come out to watch them. As a result, only 41 games of their 154-game schedule were in Cleveland. They would have played more on the road, but they couldn't. The fed up fans in other cities made the Spiders go home.

Fittingly, the Spiders ended the season by dropping 40 of their last 41 games. In their final game, they recruited a hotel clerk as their pitcher. In true Spider tradition, he lost to the Cincinnati Reds 19–3.

The following year, the league voted to reduce the number of teams. To no one's surprise, the Spiders were stomped out of existence.

PHILADELPHIA ATHLETICS
1916

Two years after winning the pennant, manager Connie Mack did one of his regular housecleanings. In the process, he swept out his talented stars. He did it to make room for rookies and rejects willing to play for pennies.

He got what he paid for. These abominable A's ended the 1916 season with a sickening 36–117 record. Their winning percentage was .235—the worst in modern history. They finished 54½ games out of first. Even the seventh-place Senators were 40 games ahead of them.

More than anything else, it was terrible pitching that turned the A's into F's. One of the stars Mack kept was right-hander Bullet Joe Bush. Bullet Joe was totally embarrassed. Forced to take his regular turn on the mound, he lost 22 games. Teammate Elmer Myers barely nosed Bush out for most losses in the league with 23. Hurler Jack Nabors won the first game he pitched that season. Then Nabors lost his next 19 decisions. It earned him a place in the record book. He tied for the most consecutive games lost in a season.

After his awful record-breaking season, Nabors dropped out of sight. Unfortunately, Mack and the rest of the A's didn't. The next year, the A's finished last again, 44½ games back.

PHILADELPHIA PHILLIES
1961

It was a rainy night in Philadelphia, but a wildly happy mob of baseball fans filled International Airport. With victory banners and brass bands, they had come to welcome home the Phils.

Manager Gene Mauch was carried through the terminal on the fans' shoulders. Mauch was full of emotion. He told the roaring crowd that it was "hard to believe how these kids kept battling through all those games. It's something to make these players proud."

A pennant winner come home? A World Series champ? No-o-o-o!

After four straight winless weeks, the Phillies had finally won a game. When the victory drought ended, they had established a modern major league record by losing 23 games in a row.

The Phillies weren't just a so-so team on a bad luck roll. They stunk up the league all year long with a 47–107 record.

They became famous for consistently blowing close games they should have won. Take the game that tied the record of 20 consecutive losses. The Phillies lost a two-run lead in the eighth inning against the Braves. The game was forced into extra frames. In the tenth, they wriggled out of a bases-loaded jam with a nifty double play. In the next inning, the Phils met the challenge head-on. They did what they usually did best. On two walks and an error, they gave the game away.

The Phillies set a new record for futility the next day. Lew Burdette of the Braves buzz-sawed them on a three-hitter. The frustration continued in loss number 22. The Phillies whacked 12 hits but left men on base in every inning. In the ninth, they wasted a no-out, bases-loaded opportunity—before losing 4–3.

But all bad things must come to an end. After losing the first game of a doubleheader, they finally tasted victory. On August 20, the Phils beat the Braves 7–4 behind pitcher John Buzhardt. Nobody was happier than Buzhardt over his fourth win of the season. He was the last Phillies pitcher to win a game before the losing streak started on July 28.

A footnote to the great Philly Flop: Pitching ace Robin Roberts started the 1961 season with 233 career wins. He finished the year with 234 wins.

NEW YORK METS
1962

The Mets were the most hilarious bunch of has-beens and never-would-be's ever seen on a diamond. They had a lineup that even Rodney Dangerfield couldn't respect.

With all the wrong stuff, they stumbled to a shameful 40–120 season. Manager Casey Stengel marveled: "They've shown me ways to lose I never knew existed."

It took them 10 games to figure out how to win. But within a few weeks, they went on a 17-game losing streak. Thus, their place in infamy was assured.

The Mets had two problems. Either they were too young or too old. The over-the-hill gang included such players as Richie Ashburn, Gus Bell, Wilmer "Vinegar Bend" Mizell, Gil Hodges, and 40-year-old Gene Woodling. Woodling later said his favorite memory of the season was going home when it was all over.

Then there was veteran Don Zimmer, the Met third baseman. Early in the season, he went 0 for 34 at the plate. Finally, he broke out of his slump with a single. The Mets quickly traded him to the Reds. They wanted to deal Zimmer while he was hot. In exchange, the Mets received Cliff Cook, a promising power hitter and third sacker. There was only one problem. Cook had a slipped disk in his back and couldn't bend over.

That year, the Mets went through nine catchers. Each, it seemed, had his own specialty. Choo Choo Coleman could catch but he couldn't hit or throw. Hobie Landrith could hit but he couldn't catch or throw. Harry Chiti couldn't do any of the above. New York had obtained him from Cleveland for a player to be named later. When they discovered Chiti was no major league player—even by Met standards—they unloaded him. And since they owed Cleveland a player, they sent Chiti. Only the Mets could have pulled off a deal like this—trading Chiti for himself.

So many players came and went that the clubhouse looked like Grand Central Station. Another early season trade brought the team a balding, veteran first baseman. His good years—if you could call them good—were behind him. His name was Marvelous Marv Throneberry.

Throneberry could make the worst out of any situation. It wasn't that he was such a bad first baseman. He just had trouble handling throws, judging pop-ups, and fielding grounders. But the fans loved him anyway, and they gave him the title of Mr. Met. He stood for everything that was wrong with the team. Speaking to the fans between games of a doubleheader, he said, "I'd tell you a few jokes, but there are already plenty of comedians around here."

The 1962 Mets finished in tenth place. They were the first team in modern National League history to do so. Their pitching staff led the way. They coughed up 192 homers, 1,577 hits, and 801 earned runs. Pitcher Jay Hook contributed 137 of those tallies all by himself. Hook was a graduate engineer. He had a much easier time explaining the curve ball than throwing one.

On the final game of the season, the Mets lost to the Cubs 5–1. The contest was low-lighted by their becoming victims of an eighth-inning triple play. Afterward, Stengel, who had enjoyed many a happy day as a Yankee skipper, lamented, "I won with this club what I used to lose."

HOLEY MITTS!

You can tell who they are by their first initial. It's "E," as in Error. These fabulous fumblers somehow get to the bigs with holes in their gloves. They catch more boos than balls—which they handle like grenades. They boot so many balls they belong in soccer instead of baseball. For "The Most Inept Fielding Performances," The Baseball Hall of SHAME inducts the following:

SMEAD JOLLEY
Outfielder ● Chicago–Boston, A.L. ● 1930–33

Smead Jolley was one of the world's worst outfielders. Even Jolley agreed.

He sealed his reputation by making three errors on a single play. Jolley was playing right field against the Athletics in Philadelphia when Bing Miller smashed a single. To the dismay of the White Sox, it headed right for Jolley.

As expected, the ball rolled through his legs for

16

error number one. Jolley spun around to play the carom off the wall. To no one's surprise, the ball scooted back through his legs. Error number two. Jolley could have quit while he was ahead, but he didn't. Instead, he seized the moment and landed himself in the twilight zone of fielding. He picked up the ball and heaved it over the third baseman's head. Error number three. Meanwhile, Bing Miller circled the bases and scored.

It's shocking, but Jolley's incredible feat never made the record books. The official scorer refused to believe any major leaguer could commit such a fielding folly. He charged Jolley with only two errors, robbing him of an official record. It would have been the worst single fielding play in baseball history.

Jolley went on to distinguish himself anyway—in Boston. When he was traded to the Red Sox, he had trouble with Fenway Park. Back then, some parks had embankments against the outfield fences. That was before warning tracks were installed. At the time, Fenway had a ten-foot incline in left field. To Jolley it was as awesome as Mount Everest. His coaches were frustrated. For days, they hit fungoes to left while Jolley ran up the hill making catches.

Jolley's next start in left was his chance to show he could handle the incline. It was a game against the Washington Senators. A long fly ball was hit to left and Jolley took off. He ran easily up the incline and turned around to make the catch. That's when he realized he had overrun the ball. Jolley started back down the incline but tripped and fell flat on his face. Before Jolley staggered to his feet, the batter was standing on third.

Jolley went back to the dugout cussing at his coaches. "Fine bunch, you guys," he complained. "For ten days you teach me how to go up the hill, but none of you has the brains to teach me how to come down!"

DICK STUART

First Baseman • Philadelphia–Pittsburgh–New York–
Los Angeles, N.L. • California–Boston, A.L.
1958–69

Dick Stuart collected almost as many nicknames during his career as he did errors. Stuart is remembered as "Dr. Strangeglove," "Stonefingers," and "Clank." That's because of the sound the ball made bouncing off his hands.

Dick Stuart muffs another grounder and shows why he's nicknamed Dr. Stangeglove.
AP/WIDE WORLD PHOTOS

He not only deserved the nicknames, he was proud of them. Stuart ordered a special license plate for his car. It read "E–3." It was a touch of class that only a true Hall of SHAMER could appreciate.

Stuart knew he wouldn't make the record books with his hitting. He didn't have that much talent. Instead, he decided to specialize in one area—errors.

For seven straight years, from 1958 through 1964, Stuart either led or tied for the lead in errors for a season by a first baseman. It was a low mark that still hasn't been challenged.

Stuart basked in his notoriety. "Errors are part of my image," he used to brag. "One night in Pittsburgh, thirty thousand fans gave me a standing ovation when I caught a hot dog wrapper on the fly."

ANDY PAFKO
Outfielder • Chicago, N.L. • April 30, 1949

Andy Pafko was known for his diving lunges for Texas Leaguers and sinking line drives. Sometimes he caught them and came up smelling like a rose. Other times he missed them and just came up smelling. Then there was the time he lost the catch, his head, and the game.

The Cubs held a 3–2 lead over the Cardinals at Wrigley Field. The Cards had a man on first in the top of the ninth inning with two out. St. Louis batter Rocky Nelson hit a low liner to center field. Pafko raced in on a dead run. Making a diving somersault, he appeared to snag the ball for the final out. He held up the ball to show the cheering crowd. Then his joy turned to shock. Second base umpire Al Barlick signaled no catch.

Pafko was furious. He raced over to Barlick and shouted loudly that he had made the catch. Barlick shook his head. Pafko was intent on arguing. So intent, in fact, that he forgot the ball in his glove was still in play.

As Pafko ranted and raved, the runner on first scored the tying run. Meanwhile, Rocky Nelson didn't even slow down. He passed the Pafko-Barlick debate at second. Then Nelson made the turn at third and headed for home. By now, the other Cubs were screaming at Pafko to throw the ball. Finally the message sank in. In desperation, Pafko fired the ball to the plate. But it popped out of the catcher's mitt. Nelson slid across the plate with the winning run.

Thanks to Pafko's lapse, his team lost—on an inside-the-glove home run.

BILL MELTON
Third Baseman • Chicago–California–Cleveland, A.L.
1968–77

Bill Melton was one of those "good hit, no field" players. He could drive in three runs in a game with his bat. Then he'd give up four runs with his fielding.

In 1970, Melton played for the White Sox. His first month was one of the most embarrassing of any major leaguer. He committed a whopping ten errors in the Sox's first 24 games.

That would have been bad enough, but the broken nose he suffered in a May 7 game in Baltimore was worse. First, he fumbled a routine grounder in the third inning. It was his eleventh error of the season. But the final blow came three innings later.

Melton camped under a high foul pop-up, ready to make a routine catch. Routine, that is, for most fielders. In typical Melton fashion, the ball struck the heel of his glove. Then it smashed into his nose. He went down like a poled ox, knocked unconscious for a couple of minutes.

The official scorer had no choice but to add insult to injury: "It's got to be another error. There's no other way you can call it."

As Melton regained consciousness and was placed in the ambulance, he muttered, "The way things are going this had to happen. I'm not surprised." Neither were his teammates.

JOE DIMAGGIO
Outfielder ● New York, A.L. ● July 30, 1951

In 13 years in baseball, Joe DiMaggio never suffered a mental lapse on the field. Except once.

"The Yankee Clipper" had played in 1,684 regular season games, 45 World Series contests and ten All-Star games. In all that time, he had never been known to throw to the wrong base. He'd never tried for an extra base without having a good chance of reaching safely. He'd never been guilty of daydreaming in the outfield. DiMaggio was the thinking man's ball player. His teammates and fans counted on him for his rock-solid dependability. Then, in his 1,685th game, he committed an embarrassing blunder.

It came at the worst possible time. In the top of the eighth inning, Detroit led New York, 3–2. Tigers star George Kell was on second base with one out.

The next batter, Steve Souchock, flied to deep center. DiMaggio made the catch—of course. But unbelievably, Joe leisurely started trotting in with the ball. Mistakenly, he thought that there were three outs. But Kell knew differently. He tagged up at second and headed toward third. Coach Dick Bartell waved him around. By the time DiMaggio woke up from his mental fog, Kell was heading for home. Kell could run only a little faster than a snail. But DiMaggio's blunder allowed him to score from second base on an outfield fly.

The 39,684 fans gasped in disbelief. Joe DiMaggio, the closest thing to a perfect player, had pulled a boner. It had put the home team down by two runs, 4–2. And only two innings were left to play.

Joltin' Joe was ashamed. He knew there was only one way to make up for his mistake. In the bottom of the ninth inning, after the Yankees had tied the score, he drove in the winning run.

HITLESS WONDERS

*Every team has lousy hitters—guys who cele-
brate if they go 1-for-5. They hit for averages that
aren't even good for bowling. These players
couldn't hit the floor if they fell out of bed. They
would strike out trying to hit the ball off a T-ball
stand. For "The Crummiest Batting Performances," The Baseball Hall of SHAME inducts
the following:*

BOB BUHL
Pitcher ● Milwaukee–Chicago–Pittsburgh, N.L.
1953–67

Bob Buhl is the idol of hitless wonders everywhere. He
once went 0 for 1962. In that year, he went to the plate
70 times. And 70 times he failed to get so much as a
scratch single.

Buhl was an awful batter. How awful? He received
standing ovations for hitting foul tips. But he lasted 14
years in the majors with a .089 career batting average.

However, Buhl did swat some extra base hits. One in 1956, and another in 1958.

Batterless Buhl is best remembered for his hitless streak. It started with the Braves in 1961 and ended with the Cubs in 1963. During that time, Buhl had 88 at-bats in 42 games without a hit. Of course, he set a major league record.

If Mother Nature hadn't stepped in, he could have kept the streak going. But on May 8, 1963, at Wrigley Field, Buhl hit a pop-up. A gust of wind blew it out of reach of the third baseman and shortstop. They tripped over each other going after the ball and it fell for a single.

"They wanted to stop the game and give me the ball," Buhl said. Buhl looked at his career with the eye of a true loser: "The hits I had were accidental, really. I tried everything. I was a right-hander but I tried batting left-handed for a while. That didn't work. The only thing I didn't try was an ironing board.

"I hope my record stands. I think it should. I don't think anyone would want to break it."

BILL BERGEN
Cincinnati–Brooklyn, N.L. • 1901–11

Bill Bergen's batting has withstood the detest of time. In almost a century, no regular major leaguer has had a worse career average.

The big mystery about Bergen is how he lasted 11 seasons in the bigs.

During his career, Bergen played in 947 games. Only once in all that time did he hit over .200. That was in 1903, when he surged to a lofty .227. In all of his

Catcher Bill Bergen owns the worst career batting average in major league history.

3,028 times at bat, Bergen hit only two homers. In 1909, he appeared in the most games of his career, 112, and hit an embarrassing .139.

Bergen's lifetime batting average was a mere .170. Actually, it should have been lower. During part of his career, walks counted as hits.

GEORGE HARPER
Outfielder • Cincinnati, N.L. • Spring, 1922

George Harper shamed hitters everywhere. He did it by slinking back to the dugout before his turn at bat was over.

Harper was with Cincinnati when they met the Washington Senators in Tampa in a spring-training game. For many of the Reds, it was their first close-up look at fireballing pitcher Walter Johnson. For some, it was too close. Even though Johnson was near the end of his career, his fastball was still a fearsome sight to fainthearted batters. And Harper was among the faintest of the faint.

His first time up against Johnson, Harper didn't even get the bat off his shoulder. The ball whizzed by him as umpire Bill Klem called, "Strike one!" Harper stepped out of the batter's box and shook his head in amazement. Then he moved back into his stance. Harper had hardly planted his feet when another pitch zipped past him. Klem hollered, "Strike two!" That was enough. Harper turned and walked toward the dugout.

"Wait," Klem said. "You still have one strike left."

"I don't want it," the white-faced Harper answered as he headed straight for the dugout.

George Harper "strikes out" on only two pitches.
GEORGE BRACE PHOTO

MARIO MENDOZA
Infielder • Pittsburgh, N.L.; Seattle–Texas, A.L.
1974–82

Mario Mendoza wasn't really a bad hitter. He was terrible. His name lives on because he left a legacy like no other banjo hitter. He gave the game a statistic that bears his name—the "Mendoza Line." It has become a part of baseball's lingo. All big leaguers fear and shun the "Mendoza Line."

During his brief career, Mendoza had a lifetime average of just .215. When the Rangers released him in 1982, it was naturally because of his batting. His average was so low you needed a magnifying glass to see it—.118.

Kansas City star George Brett gets the credit for making Mendoza memorable. "The first thing I look for [in the listing of batting averages] in the Sunday papers is to see who's below the Mendoza line," Brett said. Thus, the Mendoza Line was born. It's the bottom line no self-respecting batter ever hopes to cross.

JOE PIGNATANO
Catcher • New York, N.L. • Sept. 30, 1962

Joe Pignatano ended his unspectacular six-year career in a spectacular way. It happened on a dreary, damp day during a dull, boring game. The Mets were playing the Cubs in Chicago. In his last appearance as a major leaguer, Pignatano hit into a triple play.

Already losing 5–1, the Mets made a feeble attempt at a comeback. Sammy Drake was on second, and Richie Ashburn was on first. It was the eighth inning, with nobody out. Pignatano was appearing in only his 27th game of the year. He swung late on a fastball and blooped it. To the runners, it looked like a broken bat single to the right of second base. Drake and Ashburn were off and running. But Cubs second baseman Ken Hubbs caught the ball easily for one out. He flipped the ball to first baseman Ernie Banks to double off Ashburn. Banks fired to second, to nab Drake for the third out. A triple play! What an ending to a career.

JOE TORRE
Third Baseman ● New York, N.L. ● July 21, 1975

Four times Joe Torre came to bat in this game. Four times he grounded into a double play.

No one had ever done that before in the National League. But the dubious feat did equal an American League record. It was shared by Goose Goslin of the 1934 Detroit Tigers and Mike Kreevich of the 1939 Chicago White Sox.

Torre's performance was worse because of what he did to his teammate, second baseman Felix Millan. Hitting ahead of Torre, Millan smacked four straight singles. All four times, Millan found himself sliding into second base. All four times umpire Ed Sudol stood over him with his thumb pointing skyward signaling an out.

The Mets were playing at home against the Houston Astros. Torre was the Mets' 35-year-old third baseman and team leader. He was a lifetime .300 hitter. But Torre could not hit the ball anywhere but on the ground. Every ball went straight at the infielders.

Torre began his assault on the rotten record in the first inning. Houston was leading 2–0 when Millan singled. But he was wiped out when Torre tapped into a double play. In the third, with Houston on top 5–1, the Mets fought back. Del Unser and Millan singled. But the threat died when Torre hit an inning-ending double play that went from short to second to first. In the sixth, the Astros were winning 6–1 when Millan singled. Once again, he was erased. This time, Torre bounced into a second-to-short-to-first twin killing.

Trailing 6–2 in the eighth, the Mets launched another rally. Again Unser and Millan singled. Up came Torre with a chance to redeem himself. Instead, he not only broke the league record but he ended the rally as well. Torre slapped a double-play grounder to short. In spite of collecting 11 hits, the Mets lost 6–2.

Torre had accounted for almost a third of all the Mets outs. The Met fans were upset with Joe. Teammate Tom Seaver came up with a plan to get him out of the stadium alive. He offered to hide Joe in a trunk.

The following night, Met manager Yogi Berra benched Torre. The Mets won 3–1.

THE REAR END OF THE FRONT OFFICE

Baseball team owners and dictators are a lot alike. They can do what they want because who's going to stop them? The only difference between the two is that owners last longer. Also, there are no armed revolts in baseball. Owners have pulled off outrageous schemes out of greed, ignorance or nastiness. For "The Most Disgraceful Actions by Owners," The Baseball Hall of SHAME inducts the following:

WALTER O'MALLEY'S ABANDONMENT OF BROOKLYN
1957

Owners have pulled some low-down, sneaky tricks in the name of money. None were quite as nasty as the one committed by Dodgers' owner Walter Francis O'Malley. He promised the Brooklyn fans he wouldn't

One of the last big hits at Ebbets Field, the wrecking ball—painted like a giant baseball—crashes into the dugout.

abandon them. Then he packed up his team and scurried off to Los Angeles.

O'Malley put up a good front for most of the 1957 season. He talked about building a new stadium or making Ebbets Field bigger. But it was hollow talk. He told the fans that he wanted to stay in Brooklyn. Meanwhile, he was playing footsie with the City of Los Angeles. Later that year, O'Malley began talking out of both sides of his mouth. First he was moving the Dodgers. Then he wasn't. In the end he betrayed the fans.

The announcement struck like a bombshell on October 8, 1957. A howl of outrage echoed from one end of Brooklyn to the other. Fans and local politicians accused O'Malley of double-crossing them. The streets of Flatbush ran wet with tears of sadness and anger. Ebbets Field, the sacred grounds on Montague Street, was no longer home to the beloved Bums.

PHILIP K. WRIGLEY'S COLLEGE OF COACHES
1961–65

Owners fire managers all the time. But Chicago Cubs owner Phil Wrigley went one better. He *eliminated* managers.

Between 1961 and 1965, the Cubs didn't even have a manager. They had a committee. An eight-member "college of coaches" took turns steering the Cubs. They drove them in and around the National League cellar. Wrigley was tired of firing managers so he came up with the dumb idea of not hiring any. He decided a group of head coaches could manage the club instead. The coaches would take turns running the team.

When he started the new system, Wrigley sent out a manual. It explained how the Cubs play baseball. Everybody already knew how the Cubs played—badly. But no one could figure out how they could win without a manager. With typical loser's logic, Wrigley explained: "We certainly cannot do much worse trying a new system than we have done for many years under the old."

The original faculty of the "college of coaches"

33

was made up of Rip Collins, Vedie Himsl, Harry Craft, El Tappe, Gordie Holt, Charlie Grimm, Verlon Walker, and Bobby Adams. Cubs general manager John Holland explained how these men were chosen. He said, "We didn't want the type of guy who wants it done his way or else. We needed harmony, men who can be overruled and not take it personally." In other words, the Cub management wanted eight flavors of Jell-O.

Needless to say, the experiment was a big flop. Without firm, steady leadership, chaos ruled in the dugout. Each head coach took over in rotation. Each one brought a different style of play and a different lineup. The only thing that didn't change was the end result. The Cubs kept right on losing.

RAY KROC'S PUBLIC SCATHING OF HIS TEAM
April 9, 1974

Ray Kroc founded McDonald's and gave America fast food. He also set a speed record for losing fans and turning off players.

After only four games as owner of the San Diego Padres, the hamburger tycoon had a major beef over his team's poor performance on the field. The Padres were losing their home opener to the Houston Astros, 9–2. In the eighth inning, Kroc grabbed the announcer's microphone. Loudly and publicly, he tore into his team.

"Ladies and gentlemen, I suffer with you," he told the stunned crowd of 39,083. Suddenly, Kroc's outburst was interrupted by a streaker on the field. "Get that streaker out of here!" Kroc screamed into the microphone. "Throw him in jail!"

After the comic relief subsided, Kroc returned to his tirade over the team. "I've never seen such stupid baseball playing in my life," he declared. Kroc's tantrum had a definite effect on the Padres that year. They lost 102 games.

TED TURNER'S MANAGING
FOR A DAY
May 11, 1977

Braves owner Ted Turner thought wearing a uniform would make him a manager. All it did was embarrass his players and insult the game.

Sad-faced Braves owner Ted Turner learns how lonely it is to be a manager.
AP/WIDE WORLD PHOTOS

The team was trapped in a 16-game losing streak. They had suffered enough without becoming characters in Turner's theater of the absurd. First, Turner shipped manager Dave Bristol off on a 10-day "scouting trip." Then he signed himself to a coach's contract and marched onto the field. He was ready to run the club.

Turner showed his style as soon as he suited up. He put his pants on first, and then the stirrups and socks. Real players do it just the opposite. Rolling their eyes in dismay, the players cringed. Who knew what would happen next?

One of the regular coaches jotted down the lineup card for Turner. As expected, Turner's managerial debut was a bust. The Braves lost their 17th straight game by a score of 2–1.

The next day, Turner was ready to play manager again. But National League president Chub Feeney found a rule to stop him. It says managers or players cannot own any financial interest in a club. Feeney told Turner to get out of uniform and back in the stands. Turner whimpered, "Can't I do what I want to?" He went trudging off, grumbling, "I wish I could hit somebody, but there's nobody to hit."

Later that day, sitting in the stands, Turner discussed his managerial philosophy: "Managing isn't all that difficult. Just score more runs than the other guy."

BLIND SPOTS

Umpires are like batting slumps, bad-hop singles, and cold hot dogs. Without them, what would fans have to complain about? Fans must admit that umpires are pretty honest fellows, though. It's just that the men in blue aren't always right. You'd swear they make some of their calls with their eyes closed. For "The Most Badly Blown Calls by Umpires," The Baseball Hall of SHAME inducts the following:

KEN BURKHART'S
BEHIND-THE-BACK CALL
Oct. 10, 1970

Umpire Ken Burkhart broke a golden rule—never get caught out of position. The result? A bad call at the plate on a play that took place behind his back.

Burkhart's infamous moment came in the 1970 World Series. It was the sixth inning of the first game.

Umpire Ken Burkhart gets so close to the action he becomes part of the play—and still makes the wrong call.
AP/WIDE WORLD PHOTOS

The Baltimore Orioles were leading the Cincinnati Reds 4–3. The Reds' Bernie Carbo was on third. Ty Cline hit a high chopper in front of the plate. Orioles catcher Elrod Hendricks jumped out to field it. Meanwhile, Burkhart straddled the third base line to call the ball fair or foul. Carbo was barreling toward home, but the ump ignored him.

Burkhart was blocking the plate, so Carbo tried to hook slide around him. By now Hendricks had fielded the ball. He lunged at Carbo in an attempt to make the tag. But he collided with Burkhart. The only guy in the entire stadium who couldn't clearly see what was happening was Burkhart. But even though his back was to the play, he called Carbo out.

Instant replays and a series of photos revealed that

Hendricks had indeed tagged Carbo. But he did it with an empty glove. The ball was in his throwing hand. The replays and photos also showed that Carbo slid wide of the plate. He touched it safely only by accident—when he returned to protest the call.

Burkhart's decision was a big mistake. The Reds lost the game 4–3, and eventually the Series.

GEORGE HILDEBRAND'S
STOPPING OF THE GAME
Oct. 5, 1922

The tension during Game Two of the 1922 World Series was almost unbearable. After ten heart-thumping innings, the score was deadlocked. Giants, 3–Yankees, 3. The fans couldn't wait to see what would happen next. Unfortunately, the fans couldn't *get* to see what would happen next.

Umpire George Hildebrand took the ball from the catcher and stuck it in his pocket. Then he announced the game was called "on account of darkness." Next, he marched off the unlighted field.

The players, fans, even Commissioner Kenesaw Mountain Landis couldn't believe their ears. It was still a bright, sunny October afternoon, about 4:45 P.M. There was at least another 45 minutes of playing time left.

The fans exploded in anger. One of the most thrilling games they had ever seen was over without a winner. A mob poured out onto the field and surrounded Commissioner Landis. He was just as upset as the furious fans. The umpires ran for their lives.

Screaming "Fraud!" the fans demanded their money back. The Commissioner pushed and shoved his way to the umpires' locked and guarded dressing room.

"Why did you call the game?" he thundered at Hildebrand.

"There was a temporary haze on the field," the ump replied. The only haze seemed to be in Hildebrand's mind.

To calm the angry mob, Landis ordered that the game's receipts—$120,544—be given to charity. Then he bawled Hildebrand out for being too quick to stop a game.

The next game was played on a dark, drizzly day. The players had trouble seeing the ball. But no ump dared call the game.

LARRY BARNETT'S INTERFERENCE RULING
Oct. 14, 1975

The irate Red Sox called Larry Barnett's decision a case of injustice. Actually, they called it things that would make a drill sergeant blush. His ruling certainly rates as one of the most unfair in Series history. It came during the third game of the 1975 World Series.

A late rally by Boston had tied Cincinnati 5–5. The game was forced into extra innings. In the bottom of the tenth, Cincy's Cesar Geronimo singled. That brought up Ed Armbrister, a little-known player. Armbrister was faced with the most important task of his brief career. He had to move Geronimo into scoring position.

Armbrister dropped a terrible bunt in front of the plate. It looked like Boston catcher Carlton Fisk had an easy force play at second. But as Fisk moved out and picked up the ball, Armbrister hesitated. Then he threw a nifty NFL shoulder block into Fisk's chest. The two bumped and pushed. Finally, Fisk leaped high in the air and threw to second. But because of the wrestling with Armbrister, Fisk's throw sailed into center field. Meantime, Armbrister decided to take off. The runners ended up on second and third.

The Red Sox yelled interference loud enough to be heard back in Boston. But Barnett wouldn't have any of it. Interference, he said, had to be intentional. Armbrister really didn't mean to get in Fisk's way.

A few moments later, Joe Morgan stroked a single that drove in Geronimo with the winning run. The Reds went on to take the Series in seven games. Moments after the bitter third-game defeat, Fisk fumed, "We should have had a double play on that ball, but the umpires are too gutless under pressure."

VIC DELMORE'S MENTAL LAPSE
June 30, 1959

Vic Delmore's absentmindedness caused one of the weirdest, most inexcusable plays ever.

It happened in Wrigley Field (where else?). The Cardinals' Stan Musial was at bat with a 3–1 count. The next pitch got away from Cub catcher Sammy Taylor and rolled toward the backstop.

Delmore called ball four and Musial trotted toward

first. But Taylor and pitcher Bob Anderson argued that it was a foul tip.

Since the ball was still in play, Musial ran toward second. Third baseman Alvin Dark ran to the backstop and retrieved the ball. Meanwhile, Delmore was still arguing with the Cub battery mates. Without thinking, he pulled another ball out of his pocket and handed it to Taylor. Suddenly, Anderson noticed Musial heading for second. He grabbed the new ball and threw to second. At the same time, Dark threw the original ball to shortstop Ernie Banks.

Anderson's throw sailed over second base into center field. Musial saw the ball fly past his head. Not knowing there were two balls in play, Musial took off for third. There he ran right into Banks who tagged him out—with the original ball.

The umpires held a lengthy huddle. Afterward, they ruled Musial out since he was tagged with the original ball. Also "out" was Vic Delmore. National League President Warren Giles fired him at the end of the season.

ALL CHOKED UP

One of baseball's favorite images is the underdog team that beats incredible odds with superhuman effort. They come from behind at the last possible moment to win a game or pennant. That's all bunk. The other team just blew it, plain and simple. The losers' flag should show two hands firmly clutching the throat. For "The Teams That Blew the Biggest Leads and Lost," The Baseball Hall of SHAME inducts the following:

PHILADELPHIA PHILLIES
1964

The word "choke" was invented in Philadelphia late in September, 1964, by the Phillies. They suffered one of the most awesome collapses in modern times.

With only 15 games to play, the Phillies owned a 6½-game lead. They could have waltzed to the pennant without even breaking a sweat. Instead, they dropped

10 straight games. While the Phils staggered to get back on their feet, the St. Louis Cardinals stepped over them to claim the pennant.

What made the famous Phillies flop so amazing was that it was a total team effort. Starting on September 18, everything went to pieces at once—hitting, pitching, defense, even managing.

For instance, skipper Gene Mauch took a lot of heat for overworking his two pitching aces. Jim Bunning was 19–8, and Chris Short was 17–9. Three times in September, he sent Bunning to the mound with only two days' rest. He did the same thing with Short. The pitching duo lost every game they appeared in during that stretch.

Then there were the defensive slipups. Two games were lost because the Phils allowed base runners to steal home. In another game, outfielder Johnny Callison let a fly ball bounce off his glove as the Braves scored the winning run. In that same game, the Phils' Richie Allen overslid second and didn't even try to get back to the bag. Right after he was tagged out, teammate Alex Johnson followed that blunder with one of his own. Johnson rounded second base after hitting a double and was picked off.

The Phillies won their last game of the season, against the Reds. They salvaged a second-place tie with Cincinnati, just one game out of first. They came so close. But close counts only in horseshoes.

WASHINGTON SENATORS
May 23, 1901

It was the last of the ninth in a real yawner between the Senators and the Cleveland Blues (later named the Indians). Washington held a 13–5 lead with two out.

Most of the bored fans had set out for home. The Senators were one out away from victory and ready for the showers. But they ended up taking a bath.

The Senators' batboy was packing up the equipment. Pitcher Case Patten bore down on what he thought would be the last batter. But unbelievably, that third out was as slippery as a greased pig. In fact, the Senators never did get that final out.

Washington pitchers gave up six singles, two doubles, a walk, a hit batsman, and a passed ball. That added up to nine runs! The Senators' 13–5 lead turned into a 14–13 loss.

BOSTON RED SOX
1978

After the 1978 season, the Red Sox belonged not in Boston but in Choke City.

Only July 21, first-place Boston was 13½ games ahead of New York. The Yankees needed binoculars to see the Red Sox. No one could catch them, said most everyone in baseball.

After all, this team had talented All-Stars like Carl Yastrzemski, Fred Lynn, Jim Rice, Carlton Fisk, George Scott, and Dwight Evans. The pitching staff was headed by Mike Torrez, Luis Tiant, Bill Lee, and Dennis Eckersley. How could such a strong team lose? That's a question baseball students are still trying to figure out.

The Red Sox flew high through the whole first half of the year. Suddenly they stalled at the top of the standings and plummeted earthward. They lost 9 of 10 at the end of July. Somehow they recovered to build up an 8½-game lead by August 20.

Then they fell apart totally, dropping 14 of 17 games between August 30 and September 16. Torrez, once 15–6, lost seven of his last eight decisions. Tiant went through a stretch when he dropped 7 of 9 games. Lee lost his final seven decisions.

In early September, smack-dab in the tailspin, the Red Sox faced the Yankees in a crucial series at Fenway Park. The Red Sox were clinging desperately to a 4-game lead. A sweep would just about guarantee Boston the pennant. Instead, the Red Sox were hung out to dry in a sweep by the Yanks. First place was no longer the Beantowners' private residence. As the slump continued, they stumbled 3½ games behind New York. Finally, they stopped swooning and scrambled to tie the Yankees as the regular season ended.

Boston had one more chance to save itself from a disgraceful collapse. They faced the Yankees in a one-game playoff for the pennant. But the Red Sox blew that game, too, losing 5–4.

"Our pain isn't as bad as you might think," said Bill Lee. "Dead bodies don't suffer."

HANGING CURVES

You can always spot the lousy pitchers. Their curves hang longer than punts. But their fastballs move slower than balloons on a windless day. Nevertheless, they play an important role in baseball—they fatten batting averages. For "The Most Pitiful Pitching Performances," The Baseball Hall of SHAME inducts the following:

PAUL FOYTACK
Los Angeles, A.L. ● July 31, 1963

The fans like to see home runs, so Paul Foytack generously obliged—and ended up in the record books.

During ten years in the majors, Foytack had never been really outstanding. But on this day, in five short minutes, he made his mark.

In the sixth inning, the Angels were trailing the Cleveland Indians 5–1. Foytack strode to the mound—and threw pitches that belonged in batting practice.

First Woody Held smashed a Foytack pitch for a home run. Next up was pitcher Pedro Ramos. His batting average that year was a paltry .109. Ramos teed off on one of Foytack's servings, belting it for another homer. Then it was Tito Francona's turn. He socked Foytack's first pitch for the Indians' third consecutive home run. By now, the next batter, rookie Larry Brown, couldn't wait to swing. He had yet to hit a major league homer. Sure enough, Foytack threw him a nice fat pitch. Brown swatted it over the left field wall for his very first round-tripper.

Scratching his head in disbelief, Angels manager Bill Rigney walked out to the mound. A little too late, he sent the shellshocked Foytack to the showers.

Foytack had set the record for the most consecutive home runs allowed in one inning. Later, he told reporters, "You may not believe this, but I was trying to knock him (Larry Brown) down with the pitch. That shows you what kind of control I had."

JACK CHESBRO
New York, A.L. • Oct. 10, 1904

Happy Jack Chesbro ended up a Sad Sack after throwing the most disastrous wild pitch in baseball history.

In 1904, Chesbro was a pitching machine. He won 41 games to set a record that has never been threatened. That year, the New York Highlanders (now the Yankees) fought the Boston Pilgrims (now the Red Sox) down to the wire for the pennant. They did it on the strength of Chesbro's arm.

On the last day of the season, New York trailed

Boston by a single game. The Highlanders could capture the pennant by sweeping a doubleheader over the Pilgrims. Chesbro got the call in that first critical game. About 30,000 rooters were on hand, an astonishing number in those days.

The game was a nail-biter. The two teams entered the ninth tied 2–2. Chesbro got two outs but had a runner on third. Desperate for the final out, he did what he always did in a jam. He went to his spitter.

But the pitch that had won so many victories betrayed him in the end. He threw the wettest and wildest pitch of his career. Catcher Red Kleinow leaped for the ball but it sailed past him. Boston runner Lou Criger scampered home with the winning run. A collective moan of despair swept through the stunned crowd. The Highlanders weren't able to score in the last of the ninth. Boston had captured the pennant.

Chesbro never seemed to recover from that calamity of a pitch. After that, his pitching went downhill. He spent the rest of his career trying to keep his hands dry.

ROBIN ROBERTS
Philadelphia, N.L. • July 18, 1948

Robin Roberts won 286 games in his 19-year career. He would have won 287 but he found a unique and shameful way to lose a game in his first year in the bigs.

The 21-year-old rookie had pitched eight strong innings against the Chicago Cubs in Wrigley Field. He headed into the bottom of the ninth with the score tied 2–2. The Cubs quickly put runners on first and second, but Roberts bore down. He got the next two outs.

Then came his moment of shame. He pitched as if he couldn't tell home plate from a batter's backside. When Phil Cavarretta stepped up, Roberts' first pitch hit him right in the back.

That loaded the bases and brought up Andy Pafko. Roberts was determined to get this batter. He did too. Roberts' first pitch to Pafko drilled him smack in the back.

Two successive pitches. Two hit batters. End of game. The runner on third trotted in with the winning run . . . and Robin Roberts walked off the mound in humiliation.

TERRY FELTON
Minnesota, A.L. • 1979–82

Terry Felton lost more games at the start of his big league career than any other pitcher in history. He dropped 16 straight games. Even worse, he appeared in 55 games without ever recording a victory.

The 21-year-old righthander first toed the rubber in the bigs on Sept. 28, 1979, for the Minnesota Twins. In terms of statistics, it was his best season. He pitched two scoreless, hitless innings.

Felton started his skid the following year. It took him to a record that had stood unchallenged since 1914. That year, Cleveland Indians pitcher Guy Morton had lost 13 in a row.

Between April 18 and April 28, 1980, Felton dropped three decisions. First, he lost to the Seattle Mariners 3–2. Next, he was bombed by the California Angels 17–0. Then he fell to Seattle again 6–4. Finally,

the Twins front office realized he needed more season-
ing in the minors. Felton was shipped to the Toledo
Mud Hens in the International League.

He returned to the majors in 1981 and pitched one
inning. One was more than enough. He gave up four
runs, six hits and two walks.

The Twins refused to believe Felton was as bad as
he looked. They used him in 48 games in 1982. He
specialized in relief pitching—and in throwing home
run pitches. In his first 100 innings of the season, he
served up 18 homers. Five of them were game-losers
that broke ties in the seventh inning or later.

"God's got something in for me, I reckon," Felton
told reporters. "He's supposed to be on the underdog's
side, right? I keep throwing mistakes and every time I
do that they hit it. I think I've got a snake around my
neck, biting me every time I'm out there."

Things got so desperate that Felton turned to
garlic for help. Teammate Ron Davis kept a string of
garlic cloves in his locker room cubicle. He believed it
kept evil spirits away. Davis rubbed the garlic on Felton's shoulders. Nobody knew if the spirits stayed
away—but the victories definitely did.

"Well, records are made to be broken," said Twins
manager Billy Gardner. And why did he keep using
Felton, with his team in last place? Gardner explained
that the Twins had no one better in the bullpen. But at
least the rest of the pitching corps won now and then.

If Felton's pitching mistakes weren't costing him
victories, it was his fielding errors. In his 15th loss,
Felton held Seattle hitless for five innings. But things
fell apart for him and the Twins in the sixth. Felton
gave up two singles. Then he fielded a double play ball

and threw wildly to second base. Two batters later, Felton was replaced, trailing 2–1. The Twins went on to lose 10–2.

The 1982 season was coming to an end. Gardner tried everything he could to give Felton a shot at victory. In one game, he used Felton to relieve starter Brad Havens. It was the fourth inning, and the Twins led the Kansas City Royals 7–4. A starter must go five innings to be credited with a victory, so Havens could not win the game. Felton had a great chance to capture his first win ever. All it would take were a few decent innings of relief work. He even had a three-run cushion.

Felton couldn't even make it through two innings. He departed in the sixth with a 7–6 lead, leaving two runners on base. Both scored against reliever Ron Davis—the guy who rubbed garlic on Felton's shoulders. The Royals crushed the Twins 18–7. It was the 16th and final loss of Felton's career. The Twins finally "waived" him goodbye.

THE FALL FOLLIES

The World Series isn't always all that it's cracked up to be. The lords of baseball want everyone to believe it's a showcase for the leagues' two best teams. They promise dazzling fielding, thrilling base running, dynamite hitting and awesome pitching. But the Fall Classic is often the Classic Fall from grace to disgrace for so-called champions. For "The Sorriest World Series Performances," The Baseball Hall of SHAME inducts the following:

LOS ANGELES DODGERS
1966

It was as if the Dodgers bat rack carried a sign reading "Do Not Disturb." During the Series against the Baltimore Orioles, the Los Angeles hitters had holes in their bats. They could have taken batting practice in a china shop without breaking a single plate.

Dodgers outfielder Willie Davis drops a pop fly, the first of three errors in one World Series inning.
AP/WIDE WORLD PHOTOS

It was the worst hitting performance in Series history. The puny Dodgers could only muster a lousy .142 batting average. Lou Johnson "led" all Dodger regulars with a meager .267 average.

The Dodgers further shamed themselves by setting or tying Series record lows. Most times consecutively shut out, three. Most consecutive scoreless innings, 33. Fewest total bases, 23. And fewest runs scored—just two!

Not to be out-embarrassed, Dodger center fielder Willie Davis made his own mark. It happened in the fifth inning of the second game. Davis moved in on a routine pop fly by Paul Blair. Then he lost it in the sun and dropped it for an error. Andy Etchebarren came up and lofted another soft fly to center. Incredibly, Davis repeated his performance and dropped that ball too for another error. Now totally mortified, Davis grabbed the ball and threw wildly past third. Three miscues in one inning by one player! A new Series record!

Perhaps it was best that the Dodgers lost the Series in a four-game sweep. They were quickly put out of their misery.

ST. LOUIS BROWNS (A.A.)
vs.
CHICAGO WHITE STOCKINGS (N.L.)
1885

Fielding—or actually, the lack of it—made this Series famous for fall foolishness. Never in baseball history have two teams shown such an amazing lack of skill. They made more errors than hits!

The blundering players muffed easy grounders and dropped routine pop flies. Throwing wildly in every single game, they racked up an incredible 102 errors. In fact, they collected six more errors than hits. But who needed hits with such totally terrible fielding?

Both teams worked hard at beating themselves. The nonstop error production continued throughout the Series. After making 15 in the first game, they made 9 in the next. Then it was 16, 10, 8, and 17.

But the "Boys of Bummer" saved the worst for last. Floundering on the field in the final game, St. Louis booted the ball ten times. Chicago (forerunners to the Cubs) topped them with 17 errors.

The fourth inning was a classic for Chicago's clod squad. Cap Anson let two feeble grounders trickle through his legs. Left fielder Abner Dalrymple sent a wild throw two stories over the catcher's head. Shortstop Ned Williamson fired a strike into the seats. And catcher Frank "Silver" Flint let two pitched strikes slip through his fingers for passed balls. Proof of the low caliber of the fielding is in the record book. It shows that 13 of the 17 total runs scored in the game were unearned.

Just for its fielding, the 1885 Series deserves dishonor. But it disgraced itself in other ways as well.

The White Stockings didn't earn their first victory. It was given to them. In the sixth inning of the second game, Chicago was leading 5–4. Then umpire Dan Sullivan made a bad call. Furious, St. Louis player-manager Charlie Comiskey yanked his team off the field in protest. Sullivan declared the game a forfeit, but St. Louis won a moral victory. Sullivan was relieved of his

umpiring duties for the rest of the Series. The reason?
His poor officiating.

So where did all this on-the-field blundering lead?
Nowhere. The Series ended in a tie. And in contro-
versy. Each team had won three and tied once. (The
first game was called on account of darkness with the
score knotted 5–5.) So Chicago's Cap Anson declared
his White Stockings co-champions. But the Browns
claimed the championship for themselves. They insisted that the forfeited second game should not count.
At least one fact remains undisputed: This Series was
so bad it easily won its rightful place in The Baseball
Hall of SHAME.

```
         1st Game, at Chicago, Oct. 14    R   H   E
      St. Louis (AA)  010 400  00 —   5   7   4
      Chicago (NL)    000 100  04 —   5   6  11
               (called, end of 8th: darkness)
```
Pitchers—Caruthers vs. Clarkson. Homer—Pfeffer
(Chi.). Attendance—3,000.

```
         2nd Game, at St. Louis, Oct. 15
      Chicago (NL)    110 003      —   5   6   5
      St. Louis (AA)  300 10x      —   4   2   4
              (Game forfeited to Chicago, 9–0)
```
Pitchers—McCormick vs. Foutz. Attendance—
2,000.

```
         3rd Game, at St. Louis, Oct. 16
      Chicago (NL)    111 000 001 —   4   8  12
      St. Louis (AA)  500 000 00x —   7   8   4
```

Pitchers—Clarkson vs. Caruthers. Attendance—
3,000.

4th Game, at St. Louis, Oct. 17
```
Chicago (NL)    000 020 000 —  2  8  3
St. Louis (AA)  001 000 02x —  3  6  7
```

Pitchers—McCormick vs. Foutz. Homer—Dalrymple (Chi.). Attendance—3,000.

5th Game, at Pittsburgh, Oct. 22
```
Chicago (NL)    400 110  3 —  9  7  1
St. Louis (AA)  010 000  1 —  2  4  7
```
           (called, end of 7th: darkness)
Pitchers—Clarkson vs. Foutz. Attendance—500.

6th Game, at Cincinnati, Oct. 23
```
Chicago (NL)    200 111 040 —  9  11  10
St. Louis (AA)  002 000 000 —  2   2   7
```

Pitchers—McCormick vs. Caruthers. Attendance—1,500.

7th Game, at Cincinnati, Oct. 24
```
Chicago (NL)    200 020  00 —   4   9  17
St. Louis (AA)  004 621  0x —  13  12  10
```
           (called in 8th: darkness)
Pitchers—McCormick vs. Foutz. Attendance—1,200.

FRED SNODGRASS
Outfielder
CHRISTY MATHEWSON
Pitcher

CHIEF MEYERS
Catcher
FRED MERKLE
First Baseman

New York, N.L. ● Oct. 16, 1912

People say that Fred Snodgrass lost the Series for the Giants. But blame is a lot like fertilizer. You must spread it around where it belongs. No team ever handed its opponents a Series championship the way these Giants did.

The Giants and the Red Sox had each won three games. One other game had ended in a 6–6 tie. The stage was set for an unusual eighth game in Fenway Park. In that final game, the Giants scored a run in the tenth and took a 2–1 lead.

Pinch hitter Clyde Engle came to bat in the Boston half of the tenth. He hit a routine fly to center—the territory of sure-handed Fred Snodgrass. But the unbelievable happened. The ball thudded into Snodgrass's glove and then plopped to the ground. Engle raced to second. Snodgrass tried to atone for his muff with a sensational catch on the next ball. But the Giants were still shaken up. The team began to fall apart at the seams.

The famous control of Giant pitcher Christy Mathewson suddenly vanished. He walked weak-hitting Steve Yerkes. That brought up the always dangerous Tris Speaker. On the first pitch, Speaker popped up a lazy foul between first and home. Any one of three players could have caught it with their eyes closed. Mathewson moved over from the mound. Catcher Chief Meyers broke from the plate. First baseman Fred Merkle trotted down the baseline. What followed was a scene straight out of a Three Stooges flick. Mathewson called for Meyers to take it. But Meyers thought Merkle had it. Merkle thought Meyers *and* Mathewson had it. Nobody had it. All three stood there and watched the ball fall to the ground at their feet. With that blunder, the outcome was inevitable—and everybody in Fenway Park knew it.

Given a new lease on life, Speaker singled to right and drove in Engle with the tying run. Duffy Lewis was intentionally passed to load the bases. Larry Gardner then hit a sacrifice fly. It scored Yerkes with the winning run and won the world championship for Boston.

After such an amazing collapse, Mathewson, Meyers, Merkle and Snodgrass should have gone into another line of work—the demolition business.

WARPED RECORDS

In no other game are records and titles so prized. We crown the home-run king and the batting champ. We honor the pitchers with the most wins and lowest ERA. But behind some records are outrageous shenanigans. For "The Titles Most Tarnished by Trickery," The Baseball Hall of SHAME inducts the following:

TY COBB'S BATTING TITLE
1910

There were shady doings on both sides of this classic duel for the batting crown. It pitted one of baseball's best loved players, Nap Lajoie, against Ty Cobb, one of the game's most hated. To everyone in the American League, it was a battle between Good and Evil.

Lajoie was second baseman for the Cleveland Indians. Cobb played outfield for the Detroit Tigers. They had battled neck and neck all season for the batting title. Coming down to the final day, Cobb held a .009-point lead over Lajoie.

Showing his true colors, Cobb chickened out and benched himself. He did it to avoid risking a bad day at the plate. He was afraid if he lost a few points it would cost him the title.

Meanwhile, Cleveland was in St. Louis for a doubleheader. Neither team was in contention and everyone was pulling for Lajoie to win the batting title. So Browns manager Jack O'Connor decided to help. He started rookie Red Corriden at third with orders to play back on the grass when Lajoie batted. "He's liable to take your head off with a line drive," O'Connor advised with a wink.

On his first trip to the plate, Lajoie did indeed slash a triple. But the second time up, he couldn't help but notice that Corriden was playing third from somewhere in left field. Lajoie dropped a bunt down the third base line and easily beat it out. The next two times up, he also bunted safely toward a vacant third base. Lajoie went four-for-four in the first game.

With his batting average now soaring, Lajoie repeated the performance in game two. Corriden kept playing in short left to save his head from Lajoie's vicious bunts.

On his last appearance of the day Lajoie changed tactics. He hit a sharp grounder to Bobby Wallace at short. Wallace muffed the play and was charged with an error. This meant that Lajoie officially had a hitless at bat. Browns coach Harry Howell rushed to the official scorer, a woman. He begged her to change the error to a clean hit. He even offered to buy her a new wardrobe, but she refused the bribe. The error stood.

The scheme to help Lajoie failed. In the end, Cobb edged him out by just .0007 of a point, .3848 to .3841. Lajoie's friends were all disappointed.

The unhappiest of all were Browns manager Jack O'Connor and coach Harry Howell. They were kicked out of baseball permanently for trying to give the batting title to Lajoie.

CHUCK KLEIN'S HOME RUN TITLE
1929

The home-run crown that Chuck Klein wore came courtesy of his unsporting Phillies teammates.

On the last day of the season, Klein and New York Giants outfielder Mel Ott shared the league lead in homers. Each had 42. The Giants were in the Baker Bowl for a doubleheader. It was one of those rare matches between two title seekers. But the Phillies pitchers cheated Mel Ott out of a shot at the crown.

In the first game, Klein powered a home run. It put him one ahead of Ott, who was held to a single. In the second game, the Phillies pitchers made sure that Klein would win the title. They intentionally walked Ott in the first, fourth, sixth, eighth, and ninth innings. To prove what cowards they were, one of those walks came with the bases loaded!

MICKEY VERNON'S BATTING TITLE
1953

The 1953 Washington Senators helped rob Cleveland Indian Al Rosen of more than the batting title. They stole the coveted Triple Crown, too. Rosen, who led the league in homers and RBIs, was tied for the lead in batting average with Senators first baseman Mickey Vernon.

On the final day of the season, the Indians faced the Tigers, who tried to be helpful to Rosen. They played their infield back whenever he batted so he had lots of room to bunt. But Rosen showed his class, or his stupidity, depending on your point of view. Instead of bunting, he hit away, rapping two singles and a double in five at bats.

Meanwhile, Vernon picked up two hits in four at-bats against the Athletics. Then word came from his teammates who were monitoring the Cleveland-Detroit game that Rosen was finished for the day. If Vernon didn't have to bat again, he would win the title outright.

He was to be the fourth batter up in the last inning. His teammates made sure he wouldn't face another at-bat. With one out, Mickey Grasso doubled. He was picked off when he casually stepped off the bag. Then Kite Thomas singled. But he leisurely strolled to second "trying" to stretch the hit into a double. Thomas was thrown out for the third out.

Mickey Vernon was left standing near the dugout. He had a big grin on his face, a bat in his hand, and the batting crown on his head. He had won it by only .0011 points.

DON DRYSDALE'S CONSECUTIVE SHUTOUT INNINGS RECORD
1968

The Los Angeles Dodgers fireballer should share his record of 58⅔ consecutive shutout innings with umpire Harry Wendelstedt.

In late May, the San Francisco Giants played the Dodgers. Drysdale was working on a string of 36 scoreless innings. The Dodgers went into the eighth inning with a 3–0 lead. It looked like another sure shutout for Drysdale. But then he lost his control. He loaded the bases with no outs on two walks and a single. It looked like the record was in jeopardy.

The next batter, Giants catcher Dave Dietz, ran the count to 2–2. Then a Drysdale fastball smacked Dietz on the elbow, but this was not unusual. Drysdale hit more batters (154) than any other pitcher in major league history. This HBP was a biggie, though. It meant the end of the scoreless streak. Or did it?

Dietz started toward first as the three runners advanced. But home plate umpire Wendelstedt was well aware of Big Don's record. He called Dietz back to the plate and made the runners return to their bases. Wendelstedt used a rule that few had ever seen enforced, let alone heard of. The ump told the amazed Dietz, "You didn't try to get out of the way."

Drysdale had lucked out. He had been handed another chance, and he made the most of it. Forced to bat again, Dietz popped up. Drysdale then coaxed a force at home and another pop-up to keep the now-tainted streak alive.

CRUD DUDS

*Owner Charlie Finley broke the color barrier in
1963 and dressed his Athletics in green and gold.
Ever since, teams have worn uniforms that look
like something a peacock lost on purpose. Believe it or not, players have been forced to wear
even more ridiculous fashions. For "The Ugliest
Uniforms Ever Worn," The Baseball Hall of
SHAME inducts the following:*

THE NATIONAL LEAGUE
1882

The most outlandish uniforms ever seen on a diamond
had a very short shelf life to the relief of the players
who wore them. They had to prance around looking
like they escaped from a fashion magazine.

In this dreadful experiment, players and positions
were identified by colors instead of numbers. White

was the color for all pants and belts. But the jerseys came in various combinations, depending on the position:

Pitcher, light blue
Catcher, scarlet
First baseman, scarlet and white
Second baseman, orange and black
Third baseman, gray and white
Shortstop, maroon
Left fielder, white
Center fielder, red and black
Right fielder, gray
Substitute, green; and another substitute, brown

Obviously, it was an idea whose time had not yet come. The players made sure of that. The season was hardly underway before they rebelled. Color-coded jerseys were put on permanent waivers.

BROOKLYN DODGERS
1916

In Brooklyn, nothing in baseball was ever done in moderation. The Dodgers were jealous of the handsome pinstripes first sported by the crosstown Yankees a year earlier. So they took the design a step further. At the start of the 1916 season, they trotted out in their new duds—checkered uniforms. Thus, they proved to the world that there truly is no accounting for taste.

They looked like they'd just crawled off the world's largest waffle iron—half-baked. But even that

The Brooklyn Dodgers sport one of major league baseball's ugliest duds—checkered uniforms.

wasn't enough for the Dodgers. They had to add yet another silly frill—an interlocking "NY" monogram. It was copied from the badges given to New York police and firemen for bravery. That figures. It took a real hero to wear those checks in public.

ANDY MESSERSMITH
Pitcher ● Atlanta, N.L. ● 1976

Andy was a free agent who had just signed a multi-million-dollar contract with the Braves. Naturally, he was happy to help owner Ted Turner with a shameful new wrinkle in self-promotion.

Turner thought it would be cute if Messersmith had a new nickname. After careful thought, Turner came up with the clever name of "Channel." He had it sewn on the back of Messersmith's uniform. Then he decided to give the new pitcher number 17. Messersmith was all set. From the back of his uniform, the fans could tell that the Braves' new player was "Channel 17."

By some strange coincidence, Channel 17 just happened to be owned by none other than Ted Turner. It was the super station that telecast Braves games across America. The ploy didn't last long. National League President Chub Feeney told Turner to call in his human billboard without delay.

CHICAGO WHITE SOX
1976

Somewhere medals of honor are waiting for all those White Sox who were brave enough to actually play in Bermuda shorts.

Owner Bill Veeck (who else?) dreamed up the bizarre outfits. They were navy blue shorts with white shirts and blue lettering—"to showcase our wares." The only thing showcased were a lot of knobby knees and red faces.

The first time the Sox appeared in their Little Lord Fauntleroy suits was on August 8, 1976. It was the first game of a doubleheader with Kansas City. Chicago won the game 5–2, mainly because the Royals collapsed in hysterics at the sight. "You guys are the sweetest team we've seen yet," cackled K.C. first baseman John Mayberry. Another Royal said Sox pitcher Clay Carroll looked like "a pilgrim going out to shoot a wild turkey."

Between games, the Sox abandoned their shorts and went back to wearing regular pants. Manager Paul Richards said they changed because it was getting too chilly for shorts. More likely it was Chicago's low humiliation tolerance. Besides, they didn't like wolf whistles.

The Chicago White Sox hide themselves in shame for wearing Bermuda shorts in a major league game.

DIAMOND DISASTERS

Baseball has suffered many shameful moments that fans would just as soon forget. The sport has been scarred by games that looked more like a Barnum & Bailey sideshow. Fans have witnessed moments on the field too absurd for words. For "The Most Ridiculous Games Ever Misplayed," The Baseball Hall of SHAME inducts the following:

PITTSBURGH PIRATES
vs.
CINCINNATI REDS
Oct. 4, 1902

Cincinnati wanted the game canceled but Pittsburgh didn't. Pittsburgh played to win but Cincinnati didn't. In the end, the fans lost.

The Pirates had raced away from the pack that year to finish 27½ games in front of second-place Brooklyn. The Reds, in fourth place, were 33½ games behind. On the last day of the season, the Pirates had won 102 games. They were one game away from a league record at that time for the most victories in a season. They wanted victory number 103 in the worst way.

But it was a cold, drizzly day in Pittsburgh and the field was muddy. The Reds wanted the game called so they could go home for the season. Barney Dreyfuss, the Pirates' owner, refused. He wanted that record and demanded that the umpires start the game. The umps meekly complied. To get even, Cincinnati manager Joe Kelley told his players to make a sham of things. He played three left handers in the infield. He used three pitchers who had never been on the mound before. One was outfielder Mike Donlin, who had played in only 36 games.

Kelley sent rookie pitcher Harry "Rube" Vickers in to catch. Vickers followed orders and clowned his way through the game. He set a record that still stands—six passed balls in a single game. But Vickers made his performance even more pathetic. He strolled along the way, pulling a hankie from his pocket and loudly blowing his nose.

The Cincinnati players boldly smoked cigars on the field and blew smoke in the Pirates' faces. Kelley himself strutted up to the plate with a stogey in his mouth. Umpire Hank O'Day told him to get rid of it, but Kelley ignored him.

The Pirates did win the laugher 11–2, and got their record. But Dreyfuss was still furious. He threatened to have Kelley charged with unbecoming conduct on the field. Kelley replied that anyone who insisted on playing on a day like that should be arrested. Dreyfuss was so embarrassed that he refunded everyone's money.

THE PINE TAR BAT GAME
July 24, 1983

It took 25 days, one upheld protest, and two court decisions to finish this joke of a game.

Rich Gossage was pitching for the Yankees in the top of the ninth inning. With two outs, Kansas City Royals star George Brett smashed a two-run homer to give his team a 5–4 lead. Or so it seemed.

Yankee manager Billy Martin raced out of the dugout, rule book in hand. Leading plate umpire Tim McClelland around by the nose, Martin smugly pointed out the violation: The pine tar on Brett's bat handle exceeded the 18-inch limit. McClelland agreed. He called Brett out for the third and final out of the game. The home run was disallowed, and the Yankees won 4–3. Or so it seemed.

Brett charged out of the dugout like a raging bull. Umpiring crew chief Joe Brinkman held Brett around the neck to keep him from mauling McClelland. While Brett screamed at the umps, the pine tar bat was passed from hand to hand. Finally, it was hustled out of sight into the Royals locker room. But the suspect lumber was recovered by stadium security guards and taken to the umpire's room for safekeeping.

The Royals were stunned that Brett had hit an apparent game-losing home run. "Broadway wouldn't buy that script," lamented K.C. manager Dick Howser, who protested the game. "It wouldn't last past opening night, it's so unbelievable."

In the Yankee clubhouse, Martin couldn't hide his

George Brett blows his top when umpires call him out for using a bat with too much pine tar on it.
AP/WIDE WORLD PHOTOS

glee. He had known for two weeks that Brett's bat was illegal. But the clever manager had waited to protest until Brett did something that hurt them. Said Billy with a smirk, "It turned out to be a lovely Sunday afternoon." Or so it seemed.

Four days later, American League President Lee MacPhail made things even worse by upholding the protest. He declared that although the pine tar was illegal, it didn't violate "the spirit of the rules." That meant the home run counted after all. The game would have to be continued with two out in the ninth and the Royals ahead 5–4.

Now it was the Yankees' turn to howl. Snarled Yankee owner George Steinbrenner, "It sure tests our faith in our leadership." And in a typical veiled threat, Steinbrenner added, "I wouldn't want to be Lee Mac-Phail living in New York."

Billy Martin complained that he had never heard about the rules being "spiritual." He suggested that the rule book "is only good for when you go deer hunting and run out of toilet paper.

"What Lee MacPhail has done is tell every kid in the country that they should go ahead and use illegal bats and cheat and they can get away with it."

The completion of the suspended game was set for August 18. The Yankees then announced they would charge regular admission for the game. That brought an angry group of fans steaming into court. Two suits were filed claiming that the extra charge was illegal. A court order stopped the mini-game. Or so it seemed.

The fuss continued all the way up to the Appellate Division of the New York Supreme Court. There Justice Joseph P. Sullivan called a screeching halt to all the foolishness. It may have been the shortest ruling in legal history: Play ball!

The Yankees came sulking into the stadium still complaining. But few of the fans knew the team was there. The Yankees didn't bother announcing that management had changed its ticket policy for the game. Fams with ticket stubs to the first game would be admitted without charge. Everyone else would have to pay $2.50 for the grandstand seats or $1 for the bleachers. Consequently, only about 1,200 fans showed up.

The completion required only nine minutes and 41 seconds. The Royals' Hal McRae struck out to end the top of the ninth. The Yankees went down in order in the last half of the inning.

A disgusted Don Baylor of the Yankees summed it up for baseball fans everywhere. As he stalked off the field, he said: "If I had wanted to watch a soap opera, I'd have stayed at home."

DETROIT TIGERS
vs.
PHILADELPHIA ATHLETICS
May 18, 1912

After Detroit Tigers star Ty Cobb was suspended for fighting with a fan, his teammates refused to play until he was reinstated.

When the Tigers moved into Philadelphia to meet Connie Mack's Athletics, the papers were full of strike talk and 15,000 fans came out expecting fireworks. The

Detroit team kept them guessing right up until game time. Manager Hughie Jennings didn't know if he'd be able to field a professional team. He warned the players what striking meant. They faced a forfeit of the game, a $5,000 fine, and possible loss of the franchise. But after finishing their warm-ups, the players swaggered off the field. Only Jennings and coaches Joe Sugden and Jim McGuire were left to face the A's.

Jennings was prepared though. He had recruited nine high school, college, and sandlot players eager to be Tigers for a day. He signed each to a $10 contract and hustled them into Detroit uniforms.

To no one's surprise, the results were horrible, even though Mack played mostly rookies and substitutes. The one-day wonders were still pounded 24–2. Sugden played first base and McGuire caught. Jennings gave the pitching job to Al Travers, who once pitched for St. Joseph College.

The A's, as expected, shelled him. With no one to relieve him, Travers pitched the entire game. The A's— many so embarrassed they hit with one eye closed— whacked 26 hits off Travers. He also gave up a major league record 24 runs. The only surprise was that his teammates committed only eight errors before the slaughter ended.

Mack agreed to postpone the game the next day. Meanwhile, the Tigers voted to end their strike. As for Travers, his one professional game must have been a real lesson in humility. He joined the priesthood.

WASHINGTON SENATORS
VS.
BOSTON RED SOX
Oct. 4, 1913

The *Boston Globe* called it "the most farcical exposition of the national game that was ever staged." It sure was. This game belonged in a circus clown show.

It was the last game of the season and its outcome would not affect the standings. But the 8,000-plus fans still had the right to see professional baseball. They didn't get it. From the opening pitch, the players, managers, and even the umpires disgraced themselves. They acted like amateur comics.

Eighteen different Senators played in the game. Eight of them took a turn at pitching. At age 43, manager Clark Griffith himself went in to pitch one inning. His 44-year-old coach Jack Ryan was his catcher. Pitching ace Walter "The Big Train" Johnson was stationed in center field. Instead of staying in right field, Germany Schaefer clowned around between first and second base.

Boston infielders swapped positions with the outfielders and laughed at one another's antics. Veteran umpires Tom Connolly and Bill Dinneen joined the hijinks. In one inning, they even allowed four outs. Hurlers from both sides happily grooved pitches so opposing buddies could boost their batting averages.

In the ninth inning, the Senators led 10–3. Griffith looked to center field and called Walter Johnson to the mound. Johnson threw several fat pitches on purpose, giving up a single and a double before Schaefer came in to pitch.

The Senators won the game 10–9. But the records for the season ignored Johnson's minor pitching role in the farce game. Johnson was credited with an ERA of 1.09 for the year—a major league record for over 300 innings pitched in a single season.

But years later a careful check of the game was made. Johnson had given up hits to two Red Sox players who eventually scored. Both had to be counted as earned runs. Thus Johnson's official ERA for that year was adjusted upward to 1.14.

As a result, the awesome record of "The Big Train" was derailed in 1968 by St. Louis Cardinals star pitcher Bob Gibson. He blazed his way that year to a stunning ERA of 1.12. If not for those two ridiculous hits in that mockery of a game, Walter Johnson would still own the ERA record.

THE DEATH OF THE TORONTO
SEA GULL
Aug. 4, 1983

When the Yankees played in Toronto's Exhibition Stadium, most of the local sea gulls took wing until the coast was clear. Or at least until Dave Winfield left.

The birds learned their lesson after one of them got in front of a speeding baseball. He dropped dead to put the blame on the Yankee outfielder. It was all part of a birdbrained scheme hatched by the winged cousins of the Blue Jays.

The nameless bird was part of a freeloading flock.

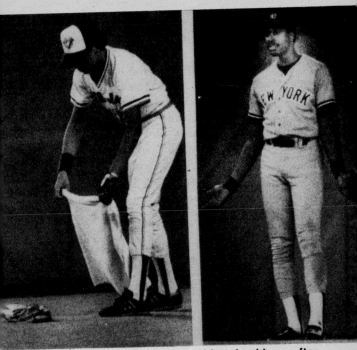

Dave Winfield *(right)* shrugs his shoulders after accidentally throwing a ball that hit a bird and killed it.
AP/WIDE WORLD PHOTOS

They routinely crashed the gate to pick up spilled popcorn and hot dog bun crumbs.

The bird in question brazenly trespassed onto the field. Maybe he thought that foul territory was for the birds. The gull was obviously bent on getting Winfield into trouble. It worked, for a while at least.

When Winfield threw a warm-up ball off the field, the sea gull stepped in its path. He was killed instantly.

But the bird had served its purpose of casting Winfield as a villain.

The crowd saw only a mound of feathers on the ground. Winfield was accused of being a cold-blooded killer. The fans started peppering him with trash and booing loudly. A batboy gently lay a towel over the late sea gull and carried it away from the scene.

After the game, Winfield was taken in tow by the local police. They cited him for cruelty to animals and made him post a $500 bond. But in the end, the bird's scheme went afoul and the charges were dropped.

Manager Billy Martin saw right through the sea gull conspiracy which tried to discredit his player. "Dave couldn't have hit the gull on purpose," Martin explained. "He hasn't hit the cutoff man all year!"

BASEBALL'S MBAS

There's an old saying that says, "Those who can, do. Those who can't, teach." In baseball, those who can't do either, manage. And sometimes they don't do that very well. In fact, they'd have trouble running a T-ball team. The lucky ones make all the wrong moves, but win anyway, because they have a talented team. But without good players to hide behind, everyone can see how bad they are. For "Managers of Blundering Actions," The Baseball Hall of SHAME inducts the following:

JOHN J. MCGRAW
Baltimore, A.L.; New York, N.L. • 1902

This little general managed two teams in different leagues in the same season. Both of them ended up in the cellar.

First, McGraw served as player-manager with the

Orioles in the new American League. But his dirty tricks on the field kept him in constant hot water. Early in the season, league president Ban Johnson suspended McGraw indefinitely because of his constant umpire baiting. By then, McGraw had led his Orioles to seventh place with a 28–34 mark.

This happened when the American League was trying to get started and the National League was trying to stop them. To get back at Johnson, McGraw opened secret talks with owners in the rival league. A deal was cut, and McGraw moved to New York to manage the Giants.

When McGraw came on board, the Giants were in eighth place. After he took charge, they never budged from the cellar. Under his leadership, the team won 25 and lost 38 for a dead last finish. Their overall record was 48–88, 53½ games out of first in the National League.

And the Orioles of the American League? With the start McGraw gave them, they finished at the bottom, too. They ended the season with a 50–88 mark, 34 games behind the front runner.

WILBERT ROBINSON
Brooklyn, N.L. ● 1925

Wilbert Robinson was the founder of the Bonehead Club of Ebbets Field. Back then, anyone in a Dodger uniform could qualify for membership. But manager Robinson made it formal by setting the standards.

The Dodgers were famous for blunders and goofing around on the field. Robinson had an idea to cut down on the errors and foolishness. The rules were simple. Every time a player pulled a boner, he put $10 in the pot and joined the Bonehead Club. Robinson figured that there would be more money in the pot by the end of the year than they would get from the winner's share of the World Series take—if they made it that far.

Great idea! But it didn't last out the first day. Robinson handed the umpires the wrong lineup card at the start of the game. He had to ante up the first ten bucks, and called the whole thing off.

LOU BOUDREAU
Cleveland, A.L. ● 1942

Lou Boudreau had a cold. Lou Boudreau blew his nose—and the game along with it.

During his rookie year as Cleveland's player-manager, Boudreau came down with the sniffles. He took himself out of the lineup but stayed in the dugout where he sent signals to his third base coach. One of the signals, putting a towel to his face, meant a double steal.

But Boudreau promptly forgot it. During the game, Cleveland's Pat Seerey made it to second base. His nickname was Fat Pat, which said a lot about Seerey's speed. Another Cleveland runner who was just as slow was on first.

Without thinking, Boudreau reached for a towel to blow his runny nose. The next thing he knew, Fat Pat lumbered toward third while his teammate plodded toward second. The only ones more surprised than

Boudreau were the opposing infielders who tagged out both runners for a ridiculously easy double play. Of course, the Indians ended up losing the game.

Boudreau scolded coach Oscar "Spinach" Melillo. He scolded him for calling such a stupid play "with those truck horses on base." But then Melillo calmly explained that it was Boudreau who gave the signal—and then blew it.

FOUL BAWLS

*Some ballplayers are also inventors—of excuses.
It's never their fault that they can't catch a fly ball
or get a hit. Something else is always to blame.
And when they need a reason to stay out of the
lineup, they're at their best. For "The Worst Excuses for Missing a Game or Blowing a Play,"
The Baseball Hall of SHAME inducts the following:*

JOSE CARDENAL
Outfielder ● San Francisco–St. Louis–Chicago– Philadelphia–New York, N.L.; California– Cleveland–Kansas City, A.L. ● 1963–80

It wouldn't have mattered if Jose hadn't been a decent
outfielder. His wonderful imagination would have kept
him on the roster.

    If Jose couldn't give 100 percent effort, he didn't

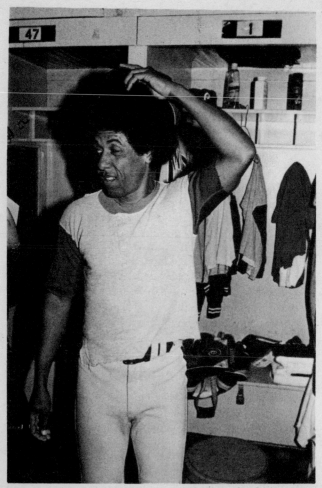

Jose Cardenal claimed he was too tired to play because crickets kept him up all night.
AP/WIDE WORLD PHOTOS

believe in giving any. So he often drove his managers crazy with reasons to stay in the dugout.

Before one road game in 1972, Jose took himself out of the Cubs lineup. He said it was because of "crickets." His puzzled manager, Whitey Lockman, asked for a better explanation. Lockman expected an excuse straight from left field, and got one. Jose said there were crickets in his hotel room the night before. They had made so much noise he couldn't sleep. Now he was too tired to play.

Jose topped that wacky excuse in 1974. He decided to take it easy on the bench for a few games. The reason this time? His eyelid was stuck open!

LOU NOVIKOFF
Outfielder • Chicago, N.L. • 1941–44

They didn't call him "The Mad Russian" for nothing. That's "mad" as in totally bananas.

Anytime a ball was hit over his head in Wrigley Field, Novikoff would back up only so far and no farther. Usually, the ball bounced off the wall and shot past him back toward the infield.

Why did he always give up on those catchable long drives? Because, Novikoff told Cubs manager Charlie Grimm, he had a terrible fear of vines! In ivy-covered Wrigley Field, that can be a real problem.

Grimm tried everything he could think of to cure Novikoff of his fear. He brought in poison goldenrod to show Novikoff that the vines were not poison. Grimm rubbed the Wrigley vines all over his own face and hands. He even chewed a few to prove it wasn't poison ivy. But Novikoff never did get over his fear of vines. As a result, a lot of balls sailed over his head.

And if that excuse for his awful fielding got a little weak, he had another one. "I can't play in Wrigley," he complained to Grimm, "because the left field line isn't straight like it is in other parks. It's crooked."

BILLY LOES
Pitcher • Brooklyn, N.L. • Oct. 6, 1952

During the 1952 World Series, Billy Loes threw more excuses than fastballs.

He hurled his best alibis in the seventh inning of the sixth game. The Dodgers were winning 1–0, but the Yankees had a runner on first. Loes went into his stretch and dropped the ball to commit a balk. Later he explained that the ball just squirted out of his hands. He said there was "too much spit on it."

That was bad, but his excuse for the next play was even worse. With a runner in scoring position, weak-hitting pitcher Vic Raschi hit an easy grounder. It went back to the mound, but Loes didn't get his glove down in time. The ball bounced off his knee for an RBI single. The Dodgers lost, 3–2. Loes' alibi for missing the grounder: "I lost it in the sun."

Even before the Series began, Loes tried to weasel out of trouble. A newspaper quoted him as saying that the Yankees would beat his Dodgers in six games. That wasn't the brightest thing to say about a team you're pitching for. Chuck Dressen, the Brooklyn manager, read him the riot act for his ridiculous statements. Loes blamed the reporter. "I told him the Yankees would win in seven," he said, "but he screwed it up and had me saying they would win it in six!"

DANGER SIGNS

Lost titles, blown games, and ruined reputations aren't always due to the players' goofs. Sometimes bubbleheaded coaching from the sidelines causes the on-field blundering. Too often the coaches take a nap while the players take the rap. For "The Worst Coaching Bloopers," The Baseball Hall of SHAME inducts the following:

JOE MCCARTHY
Acting Third Base Coach ● New York Yankees
April 26, 1931

Manager Joe McCarthy liked to think of himself as a coach. But he learned to stick to managing after pulling one really awesome boner. It cost Lou Gehrig the home run crown.

During a game with the Senators, McCarthy took over as third base coach. At one point, Lyn Lary was on first, with Gehrig at bat. Gehrig smashed a drive toward the right center field stands. As Lary rounded second, he glanced toward center. He saw outfielder Sam Rice catch the ball. What Lary didn't see was that Rice caught the ball after it bounced out of the stands. It was actually a home run. Lary thought it was the third out to end the inning so he crossed third and trotted into the Yankee dugout. Meanwhile, Gehrig rounded the bases certain of his homer. He thought that Lary had already scored ahead of him. But Gehrig was called out for passing the base runner.

And where was Joe McCarthy, whose job it was to prevent such blunders? He was leading the crowd in the cheers for Gehrig's homer—with his back to the field! McCarthy's cheerleading robbed Gehrig of the home run. Gehrig was credited with a triple. Even worse, Gehrig was cheated out of the home run title. When the season ended, he and Babe Ruth were tied at 46 round-trippers each.

After that game, which the Yankees lost 9–7, Mc-Carthy called his signals from the dugout.

SALTY PARKER
Third Base Coach ● Houston, N.L. ● Sept. 22, 1969

It was a tight ball game, with the Astros trailing the Braves, 4–3, in the seventh inning. But Houston had the tying run at third.

Base runner Norm Miller inched down the third base line. Coach Salty Parker reminded him to be extra careful of a possible pickoff. Parker's job was to do what he could to help Miller score the tying run.

On the next pitch, Braves pitcher Cecil Upshaw fired a low, outside fastball. Catcher Bob Didier, who was wearing a temporary cast on a finger on his glove hand, lunged for the ball. He caught it, but the force of the pitch knocked the white cast loose. It went spinning end over end toward the backstop. At least, that's what most everybody in the ball park saw. To Parker, the spinning cast looked like a baseball—a wild pitch that got away.

"Go! Go!" he screamed at Miller. Following Parker's orders, Miller raced for home. Too bad for the Astros that he listened to his coach.

Parker didn't notice that Didier hadn't bothered to chase the "wild pitch." The catcher was standing at the plate with a huge grin on his face—and the ball in his hand. He was waiting to tag out a surprised Norm Miller. The Astros lost the game . . . and had a few salty words for Parker.

TONY CUCCINELLO
Third Base Coach • Chicago, A.L. • Oct. 2, 1959

"Cooch" Cuccinello couldn't tell the difference between Sherman Lollar and a Sherman tank. Sherman, the ballplayer, was just about as slow as Sherman, the tank. But that didn't matter to Cooch. He was coaching at third for the White Sox in the second game of the 1959 World Series.

The Sox were trailing the Los Angeles Dodgers 4–2 in the eighth inning. With nobody out in the bottom of the eighth, the Sox were threatening. Earl Torgeson was on second and catcher Sherm Lollar was on first. Al Smith hit a long drive to left center and Torgeson scored easily. But Lollar, never known for his speed, came puffing around second while outfielder Wally Moon played the carom off the wall. As Moon was turning to hit the cutoff man, Cooch was yelling in the coach's box for Sherm to "Go!" Sherm went, but not nearly fast enough. Shortstop Maury Wills took Moon's throw and fired the relay home. When Sherm finally chugged to the plate, catcher Johnny Roseboro was waiting for him with the ball. Sherm didn't even bother to slide. It would have been useless.

If Lollar had not tried to score, the White Sox would have had runners at second and third with nobody out. They could have tied, if not beaten, the Dodgers. Now the White Sox had a runner on second and one out. They then lost the game 4–3. It was the turning point of the series. The Dodgers went on to beat Chicago four games to two for the championship.

"I waved him in," Cuccinello admitted. "I'm to blame."

Nobody's arguing, Cooch.

DREADFUL DRUBBINGS

Losing a game is one thing. But getting whipped, trounced, trampled, and stomped is a real disgrace. It's such a horrible feeling, you can't really explain it. And usually, nobody even wants to try. For "The Most Crushing Single Game Defeats," The Baseball Hall of SHAME inducts the following:

BOSTON RED SOX 29, ST. LOUIS BROWNS 4
June 8, 1950

No team ever sank lower than the Browns. They wound up on the short end of the most lopsided score in modern baseball history.

It was a long, dismal afternoon in Boston. Four Browns pitchers gave up runs like the game was a bake sale—cheaper by the dozen. The 5,105 fans in Fenway Park roared with delight, but not for the Red Sox offense. They were cheering the bungling Browns pitchers. On their way to this blowout, the St. Louis hurlers allowed the most runs in one game and the most total bases—60.

This was no fluke. The Brownies turned losing into an art. They began working on their masterpiece the day before when they were whipped by the Red Sox 20–4.

Twenty-four hours later, the Browns hurlers put on a real show of throw-and-duck. They served up 28 hits, including nine doubles, seven homers, and a triple.

Browns starter Cliff Fannin got the discredit for the loss. His pitches were hit harder than he threw them. He was shelled for eight runs in the first two innings. After Fannin fell apart, pitcher Cuddles Marshall took over. You would expect the Red Sox to pick on a guy named Cuddles. And pick they did—for another nine runs in 1⅔ innings. Sid Schacht came to the mound next. He lasted 3⅔ innings before he ran for cover. Tom Ferrick relieved Schacht. Then, to everybody's relief, Ferrick somehow got the last two outs. The disaster was finally over.

The Browns pitchers even had trouble getting out the weakest hitter on the Red Sox. Opposing hurler Chuck Stobbs collected two hits and walked four times in a row.

PITTSBURGH PIRATES 22,
CHICAGO CUBS 0
Sept. 16, 1975

It was the worst shutout slaughter of the twentieth century.

Before the first three outs, the Cubs were praying for rain and looking for a place to hide.

The fans at Wrigley Field were barely in their seats before starting pitcher Rick Reuschel hit the showers. He lasted only ⅓ inning but gave up eight runs, six hits, and two walks. The Pirates added another tally in the first. They went on to batter Cub pitching for 24 hits. Every single Pirate in the starting lineup collected at least one hit. And every Pirate scored at least one run.

The vendors were selling hot dogs to go after the first inning. Nobody was more bored by the game than some of the Cubs themselves. Outfielder Jose Cardenal was a good example. He didn't have much to do except chase down Pirate extra-base hits. So Cardenal studied the ivy on the outfield wall. "I was watching a spider crawl through the ivy," he said. "What else was there to do out there in a game like that?"

BOSTON RED SOX 23,
DETROIT TIGERS 3
June 18, 1953

There were no limits to what the Tigers would do to humiliate themselves. On June 17, 1953, they were blown out by the Red Sox 17–1. The next day, they were bombed by Boston again for another 17 runs. But this time it was in one inning.

It was like the battle between General Custer and the Sioux Indian nation.

Detroit trailed Boston 5–3 going into the bottom of the seventh inning. That's when the attack started. It lasted for 48 minutes. When the toothless Tigers finally staggered off the field, they took a shameful record with them. The Tigers had allowed the highest-scoring inning in modern history.

In the inning, three Detroit pitchers faced 23 batters before getting three outs. They surrendered 11 singles, two doubles, a home run, and six walks. They had no one to blame but themselves. All 17 runs were earned.

BROOKLYN DODGERS 19,
CINCINNATI REDS 1
May 21, 1955

It's a good thing this wasn't a boxing match. The referee would have stopped the fight at the opening bell. But this was baseball, so the Reds had to stick it out.

Cincinnati suffered the fastest beating ever dished out on a major league diamond.

The Reds gave up 15 runs in the first inning. Cincinnati forgot what an out was. The Dodgers sent 31 men to the plate during that first frame. Every one of them hit safely except for Gil Hodges. He walked twice. Before the third out was recorded, every player had scored. Every player had also driven in at least one run. Nineteen men reached base safely on ten hits, seven walks, and two hit batsmen.

Nobody understood better just how ridiculous the inning was than Reds starter Ewell Blackwell. Manager Luke Sewell pulled him in the first inning and sent Bud Byerly in to relieve. Blackwell showered, changed, and caught a cab back to the hotel. Then he went to the lounge to watch the rest of the game on television. To his amazement, the game was still in the first inning. But Blackwell didn't share his embarrassment alone. Before the first inning was over, into the lounge walked *his* reliever, Bud Byerly!

Razing the Roof

Today's round, all-purpose stadiums are really dull and drab. They're nothing like the ballparks built before domes, Astro-turf and theater seats. Those old places had style, color, and charm. Oh yeah? Some were built by people who must have hated baseball. Inside them, fans and players alike froze, fried, and generally suffered. For "The Worst Ballparks for Watching and Playing Games," The Baseball Hall of SHAME inducts the following:

CANDLESTICK PARK
San Francisco • 1960–Present

Candlestick Park has been called everything except a stadium. "The Abomination by the Bay" and "Baseball's Alcatraz" are some of the nicer nicknames.

Everybody suffers in Candlestick. Ask pitcher Stu Miller. During the 1961 All-Star Game, a 60 m.p.h. gust of wind knocked him off balance. Miller was charged with a balk! It showed the world that Candlestick might make a good wind tunnel.

When the All-Star contest started, it was a hot and humid 81 degrees. In the early innings, 22 fans were carried out with heat exhaustion. By the seventh frame, however, a cold wind was howling. The bull pen pitchers had to bundle up in blankets to keep warm.

Candlestick is the only outdoor stadium in the world that requires heating. The temperature there at night often drops to 40 degrees or lower, so the park was built with a radiant heat system. It keeps 20,000 of the choice seats nice and toasty. But that doesn't help the players any.

Then there's that wind. At Candlestick there is no such thing as a routine fly ball. Outfielders are sandblasted by gale force winds whipping off the bay. Infielders make bets on whether pop-ups will land in the same county. Once, Met third baseman Rod Kanehl raced back after a windblown pop fly. From behind third, he watched in amazement as it fell near *first* base. The players spend more time chasing their caps than they do balls. On top of all that, balls take tricky hops off the infield. This happens because the park was built on an abandoned landfill, and below the playing surface, the garbage is still settling.

In a 1983 poll, the National League players named Candlestick Park the worst stadium in the league. Is it any wonder?

MUNICIPAL STADIUM
Cleveland • 1932–Present

Cleveland fans have put up with their "Mistake on the Lake" since 1932. That's when major league baseball started there. And it doesn't look like the nightmare will end any time soon.

American League players were once asked to rate the stadiums they played in. It was no contest. Municipal Stadium won "the pits" rating as the worst. The complaints were nearly the same from players throughout the league: ". . . terrible field conditions . . . poor seating . . . sewers backing up in the dugouts . . ."

The fans weren't asked for their opinions, but it wouldn't have mattered. They're usually too frozen to talk anyway. Municipal Stadium, with its 70,000 seats, sits on the shore of chilly Lake Erie like a beached whale. But it was not built, as rumor has it, as the world's largest refrigerator.

The winter winds take their spring break in Cleveland. For early season night games, fans bundle up like Eskimos. It's so cold, their knees click like dice from shivering. Sometimes, the ushers double as firefighters and put out little campfires started by fans trying to keep warm.

LOS ANGELES COLISEUM
Los Angeles • 1958–61

In 1958, Walter O'Malley moved his Dodgers to L.A. and picked the 102,000-seat Coliseum as his temporary stadium. O'Malley didn't care that it was built for the Olympics and not baseball. Or that the playing area wasn't big enough for a major league field. Or that it was brutally hot for fans and players during the summer.

The Coliseum was nothing more than a giant oven. It got so hot you could glaze pottery in it. The first weekend the Dodgers played there was a good example. The fans looked like victims of a forced march across the desert. They were dropping like flies from the 100-degree heat.

The Coliseum seats were straight-backed benches harder than church pews. But they were a lot hotter. The fans who weren't sizzling in the sun were gasping for breath. They were the ones climbing 65 rows to the top of the Coliseum. But from way up there, you couldn't see the game with binoculars. You needed a telescope.

Baseball belonged in the Coliseum like a rock concert belongs in a retirement home. And the stadium's dimensions were the bad joke of the National League. It was 425 feet to center and 440 feet to distant right. Players cut years off their careers just walking to and from their positions.

But the real monster was the left field fence—the terrible Chinese Screen. Squeezing a baseball diamond into the Coliseum wasn't easy. The left field fence ended up only 251 feet from home plate. The Dodgers had to build a special screen in left that was 42 feet high. It stuck out 140 feet toward center field from the left field foul line. Over this contraption, they draped a bunch of chicken wire. Booming line drives good for 400-foot homers anywhere else turned into measly singles because they bounced off the Chinese Screen. But Little League pop-ups from banjo hitters dropped behind the screen for homers. The screen made baseball purists furious. There was even talk of disallowing any home runs hit over it. They should have just disallowed playing baseball in the Coliseum.

COLT STADIUM
Houston • 1962–64

There was one good thing to be said about this stadium. It didn't last long. If it had, it might have been the end of Houston baseball. The reason is very simple. Neither the players nor the fans could have survived its tortures for long. It featured unbearable heat, poor lighting and, worst of all, mosquitoes.

Colt Stadium was the first home of the expansion team Colt 45s. It had only one claim to fame. It was the only park in history where mosquito spray outsold beer. The female fans didn't wear perfume. They wore "Off." Everything is always bigger in Texas and that includes mosquitoes, gnats, and horseflies. In Houston, the term infield fly took on a whole new meaning.

Fans foolish enough to attend games sweltered

and steamed in the heat. Nearby, a smelly swamp added to the air quality problem. During one Sunday doubleheader, 100 spectators suffering from the heat went to the first aid station.

On the field, the situation was even worse.

The Texas insects were determined to keep their hold on their swampland. Swarms of twin-engine mosquitoes and bugs attacked the ballplayers. They gave visiting teams more competition than the Colt 45s.

Players also risked injuries during night games because the park was so dimly lighted. When he was a Met in 1962, Richie Ashburn complained, "If they're going to play night ball there, at least they should put in lights."

Run for Your Lives!

Some players are such lousy runners they could use a second base coach. It's not only that their legs are slow. Their minds work at quarter speed, too. To others, the base paths are as scary as a dark alley at midnight. For "The Wildest Base-Running Blunders," The Baseball Hall of SHAME inducts the following:

JOHN ANDERSON
Outfielder ● Washington, A.L. ● 1905

John Anderson is the patron saint of base-running bozos. He pulled such a stupid move that for years, any boner was called a "John Anderson."

It's odd, because Anderson was known as a hustler who made things happen. He was a daring base runner and a dynamic batter. He was the spark that could ignite a team and turn defeat into victory.

But his glittering reputation was forever blemished

by one unforgettable moment. With two out in the ninth inning, the Senators trailed by one run. They had loaded the bases, and Anderson was the runner on first.

Great players make their mark in history in moments like this. Anderson made his—but it was a skid mark into shame. As the pitcher looked in for the sign, Anderson edged off first base. Suddenly, Anderson took off on a mad dash for second. Only after he slid into second base did he realize that it was occupied. John Anderson was called out, ending the game. He had pulled off the first "John Anderson."

BABE RUTH
Outfielder • New York, A.L. • Oct. 10, 1926

The Babe pulled only one boneheaded play in his career. But it cost the Yankees their last shot at the 1926 world championship.

It happened in the seventh and final game of the World Series. In the bottom of the ninth inning, the Cardinals were ahead 3–2. It is at historic moments like this that great heroes emerge. Or great goats are born. This turned out to be the day of the goat. And its name was Ruth.

Cardinals relief pitcher Grover Cleveland Alexander managed to get the first two Yankees out. Then Ruth drew a walk. Cleanup hitter Bob Meusel strode to the plate with Lou Gehrig on deck.

Even a rookie wouldn't have risked the third out by trying to steal. And Ruth was no rookie. But without any signal to steal, the overweight Babe took off for second. Ruth, who had stolen only 11 bases the entire season, had all the speed of an old elephant.

Catcher Bob O'Farrell was so amazed he didn't move. But he recovered in time to make the throw to Rogers Hornsby. Ruth was tagged out by a good ten feet. Third out. End of game. End of Series.

"He didn't say a word," Hornsby recalled. "He didn't even look at me. He just picked himself up off the ground and walked away."

Yankee executive Ed Barrow sighed, "It was Ruth's only dumb play in his life."

MARV THRONEBERRY
First Baseman ● New York, N.L. ● June 17, 1962

Met fans loved Marvelous Marv Throneberry for his terrible fielding. But on this day, he proved that his base-running skills were just as awful.

The Mets were playing the Chicago Cubs at the Polo Grounds when Throneberry whacked a triple to the right field bull pen. Head down, he chugged around first. Gathering all the steam of a hamstrung moose, Throneberry passed second. He rambled to third, and stood there, huffing and puffing, enjoying the cheers. The fans rarely saw Throneberry run the bases. Stumble over them, yes—but seldom run them.

As the applause faded, Cubs first baseman Ernie Banks strolled over to umpire Dusty Boggess. "Didn't touch first, you know," Banks said. He called for the ball and calmly stepped on first. Boggess called Throneberry out.

Met manager Casey Stengel stormed out of the

Marvelous Marv Throneberry finally remembers to touch the base.
NATIONAL BASEBALL LIBRARY

dugout to protest. A Met coach stopped him at the third base line. "Don't bother, Casey," the coach said. "He missed second base, too."

JIMMY ST. VRAIN
Pitcher ● Chicago, N.L. ● 1902

Jimmy St. Vrain lasted only 12 games in the majors. But he left a legacy of base-running stupidity.

St. Vrain had a problem finding first base. This is understandable since he seldom made it to first. He batted a weak .097 for the year.

St. Vrain was a lefty on the mound who usually batted right-handed. But he seldom connected the bat with the ball. Feeling sorry for him, Cub manager Frank Selee suggested Jimmy try batting left-handed.

St. Vrain hit the ball on his very next at bat, against the Pittsburgh Pirates. OK, so it only went as far as Honus Wagner at shortstop. That didn't matter to St. Vrain. He had hit the ball, and he was excited. So excited that he dropped the bat and took off on a dead run—toward third base!

For a moment, Wagner was stunned. He stood there holding the ball, watching wrong-way St. Vrain race up the third base line. Wagner didn't know where to throw the ball. To first for the out or to third for the tag? He recovered in time and fired to first. It was probably the first time a runner was thrown out by 180 feet.

BABE HERMAN
First Baseman

CHICK FEWSTER
Second Baseman

DAZZY VANCE
Pitcher
Brooklyn, N.L. ● Aug. 15, 1926

This was an immortal day in baseball history. Three Dodger runners decided to hold a meeting on third base—during a game. It started with Babe Herman, one of the daffiest of the "Daffiness Boys." He hit a double that turned into a double play.

It happened in the seventh inning of a game against the Boston Braves. With the score tied at 1–1, and one out, the Dodgers had loaded the bases. Hank DeBerry was on third, with Vance on second and Fewster on first. That brought up Herman. He lined a hard shot to right for a sure double, maybe a triple.

DeBerry scored. Vance, who was normally about as fast as molasses in winter, held up until he saw the ball carom off the wall. Then he headed for third with Fewster hot on his heels. Behind them both, rounding second, came the galloping Herman, head down, arms pumping.

Third base coach Mickey O'Neill saw trouble brewing so he yelled at Herman, "Back! Back!" Thinking the coach was talking to him, Vance hustled back to third. He was just in time to meet Fewster arriving from second. Then Herman came sliding in. He found himself hugging Fewster and Vance as well as the bag.

Disgusted with the whole mess, Fewster walked

112

off toward the dugout. He figured he was already out. By now the relay had reached third baseman Eddie Taylor. He was as confused as everyone else. Taylor proceeded to tag everybody in the neighborhood. Then, to make sure the right guy was out, second baseman Doc Gautreau grabbed the ball. He chased Fewster down and tagged him, too.

The umpires finally got it all sorted out. They ruled that Vance was safe at third since he got there first. Fewster was tagged out. Herman was called out for passing Fewster on the base path.

Sighed beleaguered Dodger manager Wilbert Robinson: "That's the first time those guys got together on anything all season."

GROUNDS FOR COMPLAINT

If you study the playing field, you can spot the sneaky handiwork of the doctors of dirt. They put a little sand here or a lot of water there on the base paths. That can slow down the fastest runner. They grow the grass higher between third and home. That keeps an aging infielder in the lineup longer. In any other sport this would be called cheating. In baseball, it's called groundskeeping. For "The Sneakiest Deeds Committed by Groundskeepers," The Baseball Hall of SHAME inducts the following:

BALTIMORE ORIOLES GROUNDSKEEPERS
Aug. 13, 1978

The Orioles beat the Yankees 3–0 in Memorial Stadium on a masterful late inning relief performance. The relievers were the Baltimore groundskeepers.

In the top of the seventh inning of a rain-soaked game, the Orioles led 3–0. Then the Yankees exploded for five runs. Heavy rains drenched the field before Baltimore could bat in the bottom half, so the game was delayed.

When that happens, the grounds crew usually rushes onto the field. They spread the tarpaulin in record time to save the infield from soaking.

But the Baltimore crew was in no rush. Ever so slowly, they wandered out onto the field. Normally, rain that has collected on the tarp would be dumped onto foul territory. But this time, it was dumped into the already soggy area in left field. The crew took their sweet time, dragging the tarp over the infield. By the time they finished, they all could have collected Social Security.

By then it didn't matter that they had set a new record for slow work. The playing field was flooded.

The game had to be called. Because the Orioles didn't get to bat in the last of the seventh, the score went back to the last complete inning. Thus, the Orioles won 3–0. Credit the save to the grounds crew.

SAN FRANCISCO GIANTS GROUNDSKEEPERS
1962

In 1962, Dodger Maury Wills set a record for base stealing. And every team in the league tried every trick in the book to slow him down. But nobody was as openly underhanded about it as the Giants grounds crew.

Whenever the Dodgers came to Candlestick Park, they found a soggy bog around first base. The base path between first and second was soaked, too. It was so bad that the Dodgers gave the Giants' chief groundskeeper a new nickname. They called Marty Schwab "Swampy" for his handiwork with the hose.

During one game, umpire Tom Gorman held up play for an hour and a half. He wanted to let the base path dry out, at least to the point that Wills didn't sink out of sight.

If it wasn't water it was sand. One day so much sand was dumped between first and second, it looked like a beach. Maury, who swiped 104 bases that year, finally protested. The umpires delayed the game until the sand had been scooped up and trucked away.

PHILADELPHIA PHILLIES GROUNDSKEEPERS
1955

Richie Ashburn considered the Phillies groundskeepers his "teammates." They helped him win the batting title in 1955.

Ashburn was great at bunting down the third base line and beating the throw to first. Anywhere else, the odds were 50–50 that a bunt on the line would go fair or foul. But in the Phils' home park, Connie Mack Stadium, the odds were much better. That was because of a little bit of gardening known as "Ashburn's Ridge."

The groundskeepers tinkered with the third base foul line, so it was inclined and sloped toward the infield. A ball needed diesel power to get over that ridge into foul territory. Ashburn was usually safe on first before a bunt rolled dead in fair territory. When rival managers arrived in Philly, they went straight to the Ashburn Ridge. Then they would stomp on it, trying to flatten out the advantage. Their efforts did little to alter the finely crafted slope.

Ashburn took the batting title with a .338 average—thanks in part to the Ashburn Ridge.

WASHINGTON SENATORS GROUNDSKEEPERS
Aug. 15, 1941

The Washington groundskeepers performed a disappearing act hoping it would help the home team. Instead it cost the Senators a victory.

Washington was beating Boston 6–3 in the seventh inning. Then it started pouring rain. The umpires called time, sent the teams to the clubhouse and ordered that the field be covered. They waited a few minutes but nothing happened. Again, the order was given to cover the field. But there was no one to drag out the tarp.

The Washington grounds crew, usually so dependable and trustworthy, had vanished. Even the Senators management could not locate the missing squad. Or so it claimed.

Was there a mystery here? Not really. Since the Senators were winning, a too-wet field meant a called game. And that meant a victory for them.

After a half hour, the rain stopped. But the field was still unplayable, so Washington was declared the winner. The next day the Red Sox filed a protest. American League President William Harridge studied the matter for nearly two weeks. On August 28, he declared that it was Washington's responsibility to have a grounds crew available. He ordered the game forfeited to Boston.

CHEAPSKATES

The tightest tightwads in baseball are the ones with the fattest wallets. These owners make Scrooge look like Santa Claus. Baseball has made them rich. But they expect their players to get by on slave wages. Some would rather count nickels in the league cellar than pay for a winning team. For "The Stingiest Misers in the Majors," The Baseball Hall of SHAME inducts the following:

CHARLES COMISKEY
Owner • Chicago White Sox • 1901–36

Charles Comiskey was the Grand Champion of Cheap. His tight fist on the till even led to a major scandal.

Comiskey was so tight he sometimes made his team play in dirty uniforms. That saved him a few pennies on the laundry. Other times, he even charged the players for having their uniforms washed. The stan-

Charles Comiskey was so tight he made his team play in dirty uniforms to save a few cents on the laundry.

dard meal allowance around the league was $4 per day on the road. Comiskey's players had to get by on $3.

But he was at his stingy worst when it came to paying salaries. A few of the Sox stars were getting $4,000 to $6,000 a year. Everyone else in the majors—including rookies—was paid much more. Even semi-pros could make five grand a year at the time. But not on Comiskey's professional team.

Now and then a player rebelled and asked for a raise. Comiskey would coldly tell him to take it or leave it. The player had no choice but to stay chained to Ol' Massa Charley. This was thanks to a tough reserve clause he helped write. (After his own playing days were over, of course.) The players could be blackballed from baseball if they jumped the White Sox. And some were!

The Sox won the World Series in 1917, but did poorly the next year. That gave Comiskey the excuse he needed to cut salaries. Poor attendance, less pay, he told the players. In 1919, the Sox were winning big again and attendance went back up. Still, he refused to raise their salaries.

No one suffered more from Comiskey's greed than pitcher Eddie Cicotte. Cicotte was a consistent 20-game winner. But he could never get more out of Comiskey than $3,500 a year. Cicotte won 28 in leading the Sox to the pennant in 1917. In 1919, he was on his way to doing it again. He had extra desire because of a new clause in his contract. It gave him a $5,000 bonus if he won 30 or more games. Eddie notched his 29th victory with three weeks left in the season. It looked like he'd finally collect his hard-earned bonus. But he never got it, because Comiskey benched him. His lame excuse was that he was saving Cicotte for the Series. Cicotte hated Comiskey for cheating him. But a lot of the other players felt the same way. Several of them ended up playing ball with gamblers and fixed the Series. It became known as the "Black Sox Scandal."

But even that didn't change Comiskey. He showed the world he was a skinflint again a few years later. This time his victim was pitcher Dickie Kerr. After winning 21 games in 1920, Kerr won 19 the following year. He said he wanted more than the $3,500 Comiskey was paying him. Comiskey wouldn't even consider it. To make a decent living, Kerr accepted $5,000 to play semipro ball. For that, Kerr was suspended from baseball.

HARRY FRAZEE
Owner • Boston, A.L. • 1917–23

Harry Frazee cared more for Broadway than for baseball. He shamefully used his team to pay for his show biz lifestyle.

Frazee peddled off his top talent to pay his bills. In the process, he turned the Red Sox into the Dead Sox. His real passion was backing Broadway plays that always flopped. And he selfishly used his Boston team to bankroll his failed productions.

Frazee started unraveling the Red Sox on Jan. 9, 1920, when he sold Babe Ruth to the Yankees for $125,000 and a mortgage on Fenway Park. The fans were outraged. In 1919, Ruth had set a new major league mark with 29 home runs. But Frazee just brushed the fans aside. "Ruth's twenty-nine home runs were more spectacular than useful," he said. "They didn't help the Red Sox get out of sixth place."

No amount of criticism fazed Frazee. He kept salaries low, and sold players to the Yankees whenever he needed cash.

His personal scrimping was also something to behold. In 1919, the club held a Babe Ruth Day to honor the slugger. More than 15,000 fans came out to salute their hero. Frazee gave the Babe a lousy cigar as a gift. Even worse, Ruth had to pay for his wife's ticket to the Appreciation Day game.

ED BARROW
President ● New York, A.L. ● 1939–45

In 1941, Phil Rizzuto got a bitter introduction to the cheap side of Ed Barrow. It happened in the second week of Rizzuto's rookie season.

Rizzuto hit his first home run against the Red Sox in Yankee Stadium to win the game in the bottom of the tenth inning. It was the classic moment every young player dreams about. A bunch of happy fans rolled out of the stands to celebrate. As Rizzuto rounded third, one of them grabbed his hat and took off.

The next morning, Rizzuto was called to Ed Barrow's office. He expected to be praised for his heroics. The rookie's jaw fell to the carpet when he heard Barrow's order: Pay for the cap!

It may have been the only time a team charged a player for winning a game.

ARTHUR SODEN
President ● Boston, N.L. ● 1877–1906

Hugh Duffy was one of the great hitters in the game. In 1894, he set the all-time batting mark with an astonishing .439 average. The year before he had hit .363. With stats like that, Duffy felt he was entitled to a raise.

It was incredible, but he was turned down cold. Duffy kept going back with the same request for more money. Team president Arthur Soden kept refusing. They were still arguing when the 1895 season started. In spite of the insult, Duffy played and again hit a healthy .352.

Finally Soden backed down, sort of. He gave Duffy a raise—a magnificent increase of $12.50 a month. He also made Duffy the team captain. But there was nothing honorable about the position. According to his contract, the captain was held responsible for team equipment. Anything missing at the end of the season came out of his pocket. It ended up costing poor Duffy more than he made from the raise.

TURNSTILE TURNOFFS

Baseball promotions are a way of scoring big at the gate even if the home team is losing big on the field. Sometimes, management feels that the fans want more than runs, hits, and errors. They think the game itself can't make it without some gimmick or giveaway. But some promotions have all the class of a TV game show gone mad. For "The Tackiest Ballpark Promotions," The Baseball Hall of SHAME inducts the following:

ATLANTA BRAVES PROMOTIONS
Fulton County Stadium • 1972–79

During the 1970s, the Atlanta Braves really looked up to the rest of the division. That's because they spent most of their time at the bottom of the barrel. While they were down there, they scraped up some of the weirdest promotions ever.

The guy who thought up the wacky stunts was

Braves publicity director Bob Hope. "Shame is the only word to describe what we did," said Hope. "The Braves finished in last place four straight years. So as long as the team was losing games, we in the promotion department had nothing to lose."

Hope arranged for otherwise sane, normal people to do some strange things. He had them race around on camels and ostriches. He also had them throwing cow chips—at each other. Then there was "Headlock and Wedlock Night." In a mass wedding, 34 couples were married at home plate. They were followed by professional wrestlers who demonstrated their own brand of hugs.

One really wacky promotion nearly changed the sound of Atlanta radio. A local disc jockey dove into the world's largest ice-cream sundae. Nobody told him that ice cream was a lot like quicksand. The poor guy slowly sank out of sight into the goo. In the nick of time, the guards pulled him out and revived him.

DISCO DEMOLITION NIGHT
Comiskey Park, Chicago ● July 12, 1979

Even White Sox owner Bill Veeck admitted this was a rotten scheme. And he helped dream it up.

Veeck's partner in crime was Chicago disc jockey Steve Dahl of WLUP Radio. Their idea was to give rock fans a chance to protest disco music. Veeck and Dahl planned to set off an explosion in center field. In it, thousands of disco records brought in by fans would be destroyed. And the fans would pay a special admission price of 98 cents.

On Disco Demolition Night, fans do more than destroy disco records—they destroy the playing field.
AP/WIDE WORLD PHOTOS

As expected, the stunt backfired. The unruly fans nearly destroyed the field instead of the records.

The White Sox were playing a doubleheader against the Detroit Tigers. More than 50,000 disco-hating fans showed up. After only a few innings, they noticed how much a record resembled a Frisbee. Records started sailing through the air. The game was halted several times to clear the discs off the field. Then other debris pelted the playing area. The players found themselves dodging firecrackers. Tiger outfielder Ron LeFlore was almost beaned by a golf ball.

By the time the between-games ceremony began, the fans were primed. A blond "fire goddess" named Loreli ignited the explosion of disco records. To the fans, it looked like a signal to attack. About 7,000 charged out of the stands and ran wild over the field.

Pleas from Veeck and broadcaster Harry Caray on the public address system were ignored. A detachment of helmeted police finally cleared the field. More than 50 rowdies were arrested, and at least six people suffered minor injuries.

The field had been so badly torn up that umpire Dave Phillips decided it would be impossible to start the second game. The next day, American League President Lee MacPhail forfeited the game to Detroit.

"I'm shocked, amazed, and chagrined," Veeck said of the forfeit.

That's exactly how most people felt about the promotion.

LADIES DAY
National Park, Washington, D. C. ● 1897

It was a promotion ahead of its time. In 1897, the Washington Senators (then in the National League) introduced the first formal Ladies Day to the nation's capital. They wanted to broaden the game's appeal and boost the box office take. So the ball club invited women to attend free to learn more about baseball. As it turned out, the ladies knew a whole lot more than management thought. And they acted a whole lot differently than management expected.

A mob of pushing, shouting, anything-but-ladylike women filled the stands. Most of their attention was directed to Senators pitcher George "Winnie" Mercer, the city's heartthrob. Winnie was dazzling on the mound to the delight of his adoring audience.

But Winnie happened to hate the umpires as much as he loved the ladies. The combination of the two in the same ballpark spelled trouble. The more he baited the umpire, the more the women squealed with glee. Then came a heated rhubarb in the fifth inning, and umpire Bill Carpenter thumbed Winnie out of the game. The ladies went wild.

The uproar lasted until the final out. Then an army of angry females poured out of the stands. They surrounded Carpenter, shoved him to the ground and ripped his clothing. Some of the players helped him escape to the safety of the clubhouse. But the turmoil didn't stop, and the ladies attacked the stadium. Seats, windows, and doors were damaged, and railings were torn loose. Finally, the police brought the situation under control. But the umpire had to be smuggled out of the park in disguise. And no one dared hold another Ladies Day in Washington for years.

Who Else Belongs in The Baseball Hall of SHAME?

Do you have any nominations for The Baseball Hall of SHAME? Give us your picks as we select more shameful, embarrassing, wacky, blundering, and boneheaded moments in baseball history. Here's your opportunity to pay a lighthearted tribute to the game we all love.

On separate sheets of paper, describe your nominations in detail. Those nominations that are documented with the greatest amount of facts, such as anecdotes, firsthand accounts, newspaper or magazine clippings, box scores or photos, have the best chance of being inducted into The Baseball Hall of SHAME. Feel free to send as many nominations as you wish. (All submitted material becomes the property of The Baseball Hall of SHAME and is nonreturnable.)

Mail your nominations to:

The Baseball Hall of SHAME
P. O. Box 31867
Palm Beach Gardens, FL 33420

THE WINNING TEAM

The establishment of The Baseball Hall of SHAME is a lifelong dream come true for its two founders:

BRUCE NASH has felt the sting of baseball shame ever since he smashed a sure triple in a Pee Wee League game. He was almost thrown out at first because he was so slow afoot. He graduated to Little League but "played" his first and only season without ever swinging at a pitch. His most embarrassing moment on the field occurred in a sandlot game. A misjudged fly ball bounced off his head, allowing the winning run to score. As a die-hard Dodger fan in Brooklyn, Nash was so shocked by the team's surprise departure that he ended up rooting for the Yankees.

ALLAN ZULLO is an expert on losers. He rooted for the Chicago Cubs during their long cellar-dwelling years. Playing baseball throughout his childhood, he patterned himself after his Cub heroes. That explains why his longest hit in the Pony League was a pop fly double that the first baseman lost in the sun. As a park league coach, Zullo achieved the distinction of piloting a team that did not hit a fair ball in either game of a doubleheader. Unaccustomed to the Cubs' extraordinary success in 1984 and 1989, Zullo has switched allegiance—to the Cleveland Indians.

Compiling and maintaining records is the important task of the Hall's curator, BERNIE WARD. His childhood baseball days followed a consistent and predictable pattern—consistently awful and predictably short. His teammates called him "the executioner." That's because he killed so many of his team's rallies by striking out or hitting into inning-ending double plays.